Table of Contents

Introduction 1

Overarching Findings 5

Common Core Capabilities 12
  Planning 12
  Public Information and Warning 14
  Operational Coordination 15

Prevention Core Capabilities 17
  Forensics and Attribution 17

Prevention/Protection Core Capabilities 19
  Intelligence and Information Sharing 19
  Interdiction and Disruption 20
  Screening, Search, and Detection 21

Protection Core Capabilities 23
  Access Control and Identity Verification 23
  Cybersecurity 24
  Physical Protective Measures 26
  Risk Management for Protection Programs and Activities 28
  Supply Chain Integrity and Security 29

Mitigation Core Capabilities 31
  Community Resilience 31
  Long-term Vulnerability Reduction 32
  Risk and Disaster Resilience Assessment 33
  Threats and Hazard Identification 35

Response Core Capabilities 36
  Critical Transportation 36
  Environmental Response/Health and Safety 37
  Fatality Management Services 38

Mass Care Services..40

Mass Search and Rescue Operations..41

On-scene Security and Protection...42

Operational Communications 43

Public and Private Services and Resources 45

Public Health and Medical Services..47

Situational Assessment...50

Response/Recovery Core Capabilities..53

Infrastructure Systems 53

Recovery Core Capabilities..54

Economic Recovery..54

Health and Social Services...55

Housing...56

Natural and Cultural Resources 57

Conclusion..59

Core Capability Definitions 60

Acronym List 63

Endnotes..65

Introduction

This report marks the second iteration of the *National Preparedness Report* (NPR). Required annually by *Presidential Policy Directive 8: National Preparedness*, the NPR summarizes progress in building, sustaining, and delivering the 31 core capabilities described in the National Preparedness Goal ("the Goal"). The NPR partially addresses several reporting requirements from the Post-Katrina Emergency Management Reform Act of 2006, including the *Federal Preparedness Report*, *State Preparedness Reports*, and an evaluation of Federal preparedness and use of incident management doctrine.

The NPR presents an opportunity to reflect on the progress that whole community partners—including all levels of government, private and nonprofit sectors, faith-based organizations, communities, and individuals—have made in strengthening national preparedness and to identify where preparedness gaps remain. While the inaugural 2012 NPR highlighted preparedness accomplishments in the decade since the September 11, 2001 attacks, the 2013 NPR focuses primarily on accomplishments achieved or reported on during 2012. As the NPR development process matures each year, trends in national preparedness will be increasingly evident and highlighted in future NPRs.

Year in Review

Each year the Nation faces a diverse set of threats and hazards that challenge collective security and resilience and confirm the need to enhance preparedness. Events in 2012 underscored this reality, with a variety of incidents that related to the five preparedness mission areas outlined in the Goal—Prevention, Protection, Mitigation, Response, and Recovery.

Prevention: The Nation continued to experience threats of terrorism in 2012. Intergovernmental law enforcement efforts proved critical to preventing several high-profile threats. For example, Federal Bureau of Investigation (FBI)-led operations disrupted potential attacks against targets including the U.S. Capitol Building and the New York Federal Reserve Bank.

Protection: In 2012, the Nation accelerated and expanded efforts to protect critical infrastructure from rapidly evolving threats and hazards. For example, National Level Exercise (NLE) 2012 was the first National Level Exercise to test the Nation's preparedness for a major cyber incident using a scenario involving both virtual and physical effects. Major financial-sector firms applied lessons from this exercise series in their response to cyber attacks that occurred during fall 2012. DHS protection efforts included seizing over 2,600 tons of illegal drugs, over $50 million in counterfeit currency, and more than 50,000 illegal firearms, as well as conducting over 7,000 inspections at critical infrastructure sites.

Mitigation: The Nation's mitigation investments and activities continued to reduce the consequences of incidents. For example, Hurricane Isaac tested investments in levee systems protecting New Orleans. The storm's large size and slow movement resulted in storm surges in certain areas that rivaled those of Hurricane Katrina, but the enhanced levee systems around New Orleans withstood the storm's surge, lessening its overall effects.

Response: In 2012, a diverse range of incidents tested the Nation's response capabilities, including 47 events that resulted in major disaster declarations. Example incidents include the following:

- In March 2012, the southern United States and Ohio Valley regions experienced a deadly tornado outbreak that resulted in 40 fatalities and estimated damages in excess of $1 billion.

- In July 2012, police in Aurora, Colorado, responded to a deadly active-shooter incident at a movie theater. Subsequent investigation at the suspect's residence uncovered a complicated network of explosives and incendiary devices intended to detonate as first responders entered the home.

- Throughout 2012, large portions of the Nation experienced severe drought conditions, which impacted the agriculture sector, including crop yields, and resulted in historically low water levels along the Mississippi River, restricting interstate commerce. In 2012, the U.S. Department of Agriculture (USDA) issued drought disaster declarations in 2,615 counties.

- Throughout 2012, the Nation experienced numerous large wildfires across the western and central United States. The fires collectively burned nearly 9.2 million acres nationwide, exceeding the 10-year average number of acres burned by more than 22 percent.

- In August 2012, Hurricane Isaac came ashore almost exactly seven years after Hurricane Katrina. While not as catastrophic as Katrina, this slow moving storm dropped up to 20 inches of rain and caused hundreds of millions of dollars of damage in Louisiana and Mississippi.

- In October 2012, Superstorm Sandy (referred to as "Sandy" hereafter) challenged the collective response capabilities of nearly the entire northeastern United States. As the second largest Atlantic storm on record, Sandy triggered power outages for 8.5 million people, caused $50 billion in property damage, and killed at least 162 people in the United States and its territories.

- In December 2012, a shooter entered an elementary school in Newtown, Connecticut, killing 26 people, including 20 children.

Recovery: To speed recovery from Sandy and the 2012 drought, whole community partners implemented the *National Disaster Recovery Framework* (NDRF). In addition, the Nation continued to honor its commitments to communities affected by earlier disasters through sustained recovery efforts. For example, following the impact of a catastrophic 2011 tornado, Joplin, Missouri continued efforts to rebuild and recover. The community repaired or rebuilt nearly 80 percent of the affected structures and the city began an ambitious $800 million development effort. Moreover, in the Gulf Coast region, community partners continued to implement a comprehensive recovery agenda to restore livelihoods and the environment following the 2010 BP Deepwater Horizon oil spill.

Methodology for Developing the NPR

The 2013 NPR reflects input from whole community partners. The Federal Emergency Management Agency (FEMA) serves as the NPR coordinator, and its approach to developing the NPR included the following activities:

- Conducting research to update key findings from the 2012 NPR and to identify new qualitative and quantitative preparedness data across all 31 core capabilities identified in the Goal;

- Surveying Federal departments and agencies to solicit information on annual and summary reports, performance measures, program accomplishments, results from exercises and operations, training outcomes, and preparedness grant funding;

- Soliciting updates from Federal Interagency partners on their operational capability to meet the Goal and their progress in implementing the National Incident Management System (NIMS);

- Reviewing Threat and Hazard Identification and Risk Assessments (THIRAs) from FEMA Regions, states, and urban areas, as well as reviewing 2012 State Preparedness Report (SPR) submissions from U.S. states and territories;

- Conducting outreach to preparedness-related professional organizations and associations; and

- Evaluating progress within and across core capabilities and then sharing those findings, as appropriate, with whole community partners for review, comment, and update.

The NPR reflects approximately 1,400 sources and 3,200 measures and metrics that contribute to analysis of the core capabilities and related targets identified in the Goal. FEMA synthesized this information into high-level key findings for each core capability, representing observations on progress achieved since the 2012 NPR. FEMA applied consistent criteria to identify national strengths and areas for improvement. These criteria enabled an objective evaluation of key findings for each core capability and the identification of overarching preparedness trends.

This year, the NPR highlights a new THIRA process, which is a crucial element of the National Preparedness System and provides a framework for regional, state, and local jurisdictions to identify threats and hazards that would most stress their capabilities. Through this THIRA process, states and territories established target levels of performance for each of the 31 core capabilities.

Furthermore, the 2013 NPR summarizes state preparedness data from U.S. states and territories for all 31 core capabilities, based on the capability descriptions included in the Goal.[i] Through the SPR process, state and territory homeland security and emergency management personnel led multi-disciplinary, statewide efforts to self-assess preparedness. The SPR results show current state and territorial preparedness relative to desired levels of performance outlined in their THIRAs. The SPR assessment also highlights state and territorial perspectives on addressing identified gaps.

As preparedness efforts evolve and mature, future iterations of the NPR will increasingly reflect quantitative performance data and assessment results, as well as qualitative program accomplishments that align with the Goal.

Report Organization

In total, the NPR identifies 65 key findings. Eight of these key findings focus on overarching national trends. The remaining sections present 57 key findings that relate to the 31 core capabilities from the Goal. Each core capability narrative has a set of common elements, illustrated in Figure 1 and described below, providing consistency throughout the document.

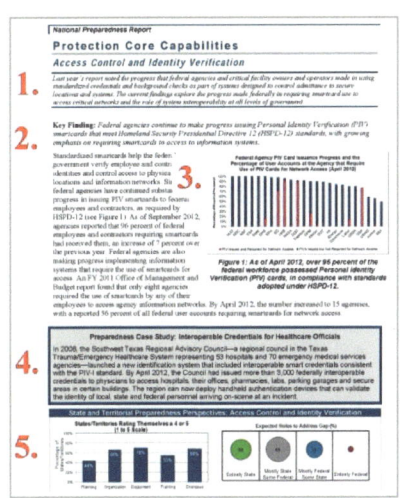

Figure 1: Narratives for each core capability in the NPR use a common organizational structure.

1. Each core capability section begins with the capability name and a brief summary of the relationship between the previous year's findings and current key findings.

2. The main text for each core capability includes key findings, which are supported by a discussion of relevant qualitative and quantitative information.

3. As available, core capability sections include maps, charts, and graphs.

4. As available, core capability sections include preparedness case studies, which highlight examples of how whole community partners have worked together to achieve outcomes.

5. A box at the end of each core capability section summarizes statewide preparedness information for that core capability from the 2012 SPR process, reflecting the broad capability descriptions in the Goal—not just the findings in the NPR. A bar chart shows the percentage of states and territories rating themselves as either 4 or 5 on the SPR's 5-point assessment scale (where 5 is the highest rating) for planning, organization, equipment, training, and exercises. A bubble chart shows states' and territories' expectations for addressing identified capability gaps.

The Goal identifies three Common core capabilities (Planning; Public Information and Warning; and Operational Coordination) that span all five mission areas and enable success in the remaining core capabilities. In addition, three capabilities (Intelligence and Information Sharing; Interdiction and Disruption; and Screening, Search, and Detection) span the Prevent and Protect mission areas and one capability (Infrastructure Systems) spans the Response and Recovery mission areas. For these core capabilities, the NPR integrates the key findings and supporting information into one unified section. Table 1 shows the order in which the NPR presents the core capabilities. An appendix provides the core capability definitions from the Goal.

---

[i] The deadline for submitting THIRAs and SPRs to FEMA was December 31, 2012. Several states received extensions due to Sandy response and recovery operations. The NPR reflects information received from 50 states and territories.

Table 1: The NPR addresses all 31 core capabilities outlined in the Goal.

Common Core Capabilities

- Planning
- Public Information and Warning
- Operational Coordination

Prevention Core Capability

- Forensics and Attribution

Prevention/Protection Core Capabilities

- Intelligence and Information Sharing
- Interdiction and Disruption
- Screening, Search, and Detection

Protection Core Capabilities

- Access Control and Identity Verification
- Cybersecurity
- Physical Protective Measures
- Risk Management for Protection Programs and Activities
- Supply Chain Integrity and Security

Mitigation Core Capabilities

- Community Resilience
- Long-term Vulnerability Reduction
- Risk and Disaster Resilience Assessment
- Threats and Hazard Identification

Response Core Capabilities

- Critical Transportation
- Environmental Response/Health and Safety
- Fatality Management Services
- Mass Care Services
- Mass Search and Rescue Operations
- On-scene Security and Protection
- Operational Communications
- Public and Private Services and Resources
- Public Health and Medical Services
- Situational Assessment

Response/Recovery Core Capability

- Infrastructure Systems

Recovery Core Capabilities

- Economic Recovery
- Health and Social Services
- Housing
- Natural and Cultural Resources

Overarching Findings

Key finding: *The Nation continued progress in enhancing areas of national strength identified in the 2012 NPR. However, more significant changes in capability levels and overall national preparedness will become clearer by evaluating trends across multiple years.*

The 2012 NPR identified preparedness capabilities that had improved significantly in the decade since September 11, 2001. These enhancements resulted from a multi-billion dollar surge in investments by whole community partners, which gradually matured these capabilities into areas of strength. Progress continued in several core capabilities during the current reporting period, including the following achievements:

- **Planning:** In 2012, 85 percent of states rated their emergency operations plans as adequate to accomplish their missions, consistent with overall improvements identified in the 2006 and 2010 *Nationwide Plan Reviews*. In addition, 61 percent of states involved the whole community in developing those plans, including non-governmental organizations, the private sector, and groups representing individuals with access and functional needs. At the Federal level, interagency partners made significant progress in finalizing National Planning Frameworks and Federal Interagency Operational Plans across preparedness mission areas in accordance with *Presidential Policy Directive (PPD) 8: National Preparedness*.

- **Operational Coordination:** Nationwide adoption of NIMS increased in 2012, with an additional 900,000 completions of introductory NIMS and Incident Command System courses. Furthermore, 10 of 11 Federal agencies responding to a high-level 2012 preparedness survey self-reported that they use NIMS to manage incidents, and all 11 reported having the operational capability to meet the Goal.

- **Intelligence and Information Sharing:** The national network of fusion centers and Joint Terrorism Task Forces continued to mature. In addition, new national strategies and Federal interagency governance structures emerged to provide a consistent and unified approach to guide the implementation of fusion center policies and standards.

- **Operational Communications:** By Fiscal Year (FY) 2012, 50 states and territories completed development of State Emergency Communications Plans. In addition, the Nation began facilitating a transition to a nationwide public safety broadband system for emergency communications and continued development of Next Generation 9-1-1 systems.

A variety of factors influence capability levels—including asset inventories, personnel skill sets, and investment decisions. These underlying factors often remain relatively consistent from year to year, yielding gradual increases and decreases in preparedness. In individual communities, some changes in preparedness trends are clearly visible because they are driven by specific community-level decisions, programs, and resources. However, broader national preparedness trends are more complex, involving the sum of all community-level gains and setbacks, as well as national budgets and policy priorities that influence the ability to both build new capabilities and sustain existing ones. Future NPRs will document changes in capability levels and national preparedness by evaluating these trends across multiple years.

Key finding: *The Nation has made important progress in the national areas for improvement identified in the 2012 NPR, but challenges remain.*

The 2012 NPR identified three national areas for improvement: Cybersecurity, Recovery-focused core capabilities, and integration of individuals with disabilities and access and functional needs. Whole community stakeholders have made important progress in these areas, although critical challenges remain.

- **Cybersecurity:** Federal partners developed and improved national-level cyber plans and frameworks in 2012, testing them through the first-ever cyber-focused National Level Exercise. Lessons learned from the exercise translated into improved coordination between interagency and private-sector response efforts during significant, continuous disruptions to U.S. bank websites in fall 2012. A 2012 study by the U.S. Secret Service (USSS) of 450 data breaches globally noted that the overwhelming majority of infiltrations targeted payment card data, personally identifiable information, and email accounts, and also showed increased criminal use of phishing emails, account takeovers, malicious software, hacking attacks, and network intrusions. However, states and local governments continue to experience challenges in improving cybersecurity. A 2012 survey of state Chief Information Security Officers found that only 24 percent were confident in their state's ability to protect against external cyber threats. The 2012 SPR results reflect these challenges, with states and territories continuing to self-assess Cybersecurity as their weakest core capability. Moreover, 52 percent of states and territories indicated they were mostly or wholly reliant on the Federal Government for closing cyber-related capability gaps, despite the fact that state, local, tribal, and territorial partners bear responsibility for securing their networks.

- **Recovery-focused core capabilities:** The 2012 NPR noted that the Recovery mission area historically lacked the national structure and cohesive planning approaches employed across other mission areas. Over the past year, Federal partners began to implement key elements of the NDRF. For example, Federal stakeholders engaged in recovery efforts established a Recovery Support Functions Leadership Group to oversee NDRF coordination and planning. Following several NDRF pilot studies, Federal partners also activated the NDRF formally for the first time in 2012, deploying Federal Disaster Recovery Coordinators (FDRCs) in response to the severe drought, Hurricane Isaac, and Sandy. FDRCs facilitated disaster recovery efforts among whole community partners, expanding local community involvement in recovery planning and execution. Despite these advances, states and territories continue to rate recovery capabilities among their least-prepared areas. Three of the four lowest-rated capabilities— Economic Recovery, Housing, and Natural and Cultural Resources—are in the Recovery mission area, mirroring SPR results from the previous year. Fewer than half of states and territories identified these three capabilities as a high priority.

- **Integration of individuals with disabilities and access and functional needs:** Inclusive preparedness planning for the whole community requires integrating the needs of over 59 million Americans with physical, sensory, intellectual, or cognitive disabilities, as well as others with access and functional needs; children; older adults, racial and ethnically diverse communities; and individuals with limited English proficiency. Building off of FEMA's success in locating Regional Disability Integration Specialists in all 10 FEMA Regions, the Agency's Office of Disability Integration and Coordination (ODIC) has been building a larger cadre of 75 Disability Integration Advisors to guide accessibility throughout future disaster response and recovery. FEMA ODIC employs its long-standing partnerships with the National Disability Rights Network, the National Council on Independent Living, and other disability advocacy and service organizations to improve planning efforts. All seven major Federal emergency plans produced in the last year address issues with the integration and inclusion of individuals with disabilities and others with access and functional needs. State emergency operations plans also increasingly address integration, inclusion, and accessibility across the whole community. However, despite FEMA's efforts to issue communication accessibility kits and ensure physical accessibility, Sandy Disaster Recovery Centers lacked the necessary features and equipment to serve all survivors until several weeks or months after opening.

Key finding: *Enhancing the resilience of infrastructure systems and maturing the role of public-private partnerships are newly identified national areas for improvement.*

FEMA established criteria to identify areas for national improvement in the 2013 NPR, based on SPR results, performance during operations and exercises, and linkages to long-term drivers of emergency management. An evaluation based on these criteria revealed additional issues for consideration, particularly related to infrastructure systems and public-private partnerships.

- **Infrastructure Systems:** While the 2012 NPR noted that capabilities to speed recovery of infrastructure post-disaster were in the early stages of development, experiences from Sandy and other events in 2012 confirmed that enhancing both physical and cyber resilience of infrastructure systems is a national area for improvement. Stressed infrastructure systems—including water and wastewater treatment, surface transportation, airports, inland waterways, marine ports, electricity infrastructure, and communications and fuel systems—present obstacles to effective response and recovery operations. Sandy demonstrated first-hand the challenges of conducting response and recovery operations while power and transportation infrastructures are significantly degraded. In 2012, disclosure of cyber incidents on critical infrastructure control systems rose by at least 52 percent and the Industrial Control Systems Cyber Emergency Response Team identified a number of infrastructure control systems with that are accessible through the Internet and vulnerable to attack. In addition, 73 percent of states and territories rated Infrastructure Systems as a high priority capability, but it was among the five weakest capabilities that states and territories identified through the SPR.

- **Public-Private Partnerships:** The 2012 NPR noted that the complex set of threats and hazards that the Nation faces and the underlying interdependencies within critical infrastructure and supply chains, both require integrated preparedness efforts. Public-private partnerships enable government and business stakeholders to collaborate in planning, building, sustaining, and delivering capabilities greater than the sum of their parts. The partnership model outlined in the *National Infrastructure Protection Plan* (NIPP) aims to establish strong collaborative relationships between critical infrastructure owners and operators across infrastructure sectors and relevant Federal agencies. Similar efforts in other mission areas continue to progress. For example, FEMA has worked to integrate the private sector more closely into disaster response, establishing the National Business Emergency Operations Center in July 2012 as a virtual clearinghouse for information sharing between businesses and FEMA. In addition, through the National Infrastructure Coordination Center, the U.S. Department of Homeland Security (DHS) Office of Infrastructure Protection enhances situational awareness and coordinates with owners and operators of critical infrastructure during response operations. However, a 2011 assessment of preparedness-related public-private partnerships revealed significant challenges in long-term resourcing and sustainability of these partnerships across all mission areas.[1]

Key finding: *Sandy response and recovery efforts highlighted strengths in the Nation's ability to expedite resources, develop innovative solutions to meet survivor needs, and work with nongovernmental partners. However, challenges remain with the Federal Government's ability to coordinate efforts when surging resources to respond to disasters.*

The scale and severity of Sandy had major effects across the East Coast and inland, including flooding; damage to transportation networks and other critical infrastructure; power outages; fuel disruptions; and significant property damage. Federal partners supplemented state and local resources by channeling considerable support to affected communities through established response and recovery support functions under the *National Response Framework* (NRF) and the NDRF. In addition, whole community partners were valuable in the Sandy response, with the American Red Cross and the Salvation Army sheltering thousands of survivors, delivering more than 15 million meals and snacks, and engaging more than 23,000 disaster response volunteers. In addition, the National Business Emergency Operations Center shared information with the private sector, responded to private-sector inquiries, and identified and resolved critical private-sector needs and challenges. Similarly, the National Infrastructure Coordination Center facilitated communications among infrastructure partners on issues such as transportation and logistics in the affected areas, access and credentialing for restoration crews, and power concerns.

The Federal response to Sandy demonstrated improvements over previous disasters, confirming that the Federal Government has learned important lessons about the value of surging resources into the field and anticipating requirements. Nevertheless, the storm's magnitude stretched Federal partners' capacity to maintain unity of effort and to help state and local partners solve the complex problems associated with such a large-scale incident. A review of the Federal response to the storm revealed key challenges that require Federal action, including enhancing the Federal Government's ability to ensure continuity between response and recovery efforts through the NRF and NDRF; delivering response and recovery support via an integrated, multi-agency approach rather than department-centric efforts; and capturing, sharing, and managing critical information to improve overall situational awareness.

Key finding: *States and territories continue to report the highest capability levels in those areas frequently cited as high priority. Interstate mutual aid plays a limited role in augmenting the capabilities of states and territories.*

Through the 2012 SPR, all states and territories assessed their capacity to deliver the 31 core capabilities identified in the Goal. Each capability assessment includes ratings for planning, organization, equipment, training, and exercises, using a 5-point scale (where 5 is the highest rating). On-scene Security and Protection received the highest national assessment average—61 percent of responses fell within the top two rating categories. As Figure 2 shows, 9 of the 10 highest rated capabilities were either Common capabilities (Planning, Public Information and Warning, Operational Coordination,) or fell within the Response mission area. Recovery-focused capabilities and Cybersecurity remain among the lowest-rated capabilities. In addition, states and territories indicated that mutual aid made a modest contribution to overall capability levels, with 26 percent of responses citing increased capability due to mutual aid. In those cases, the effect was generally small: 74 percent of the time the mutual aid contribution was too small to change the state's assessment of its capability level.

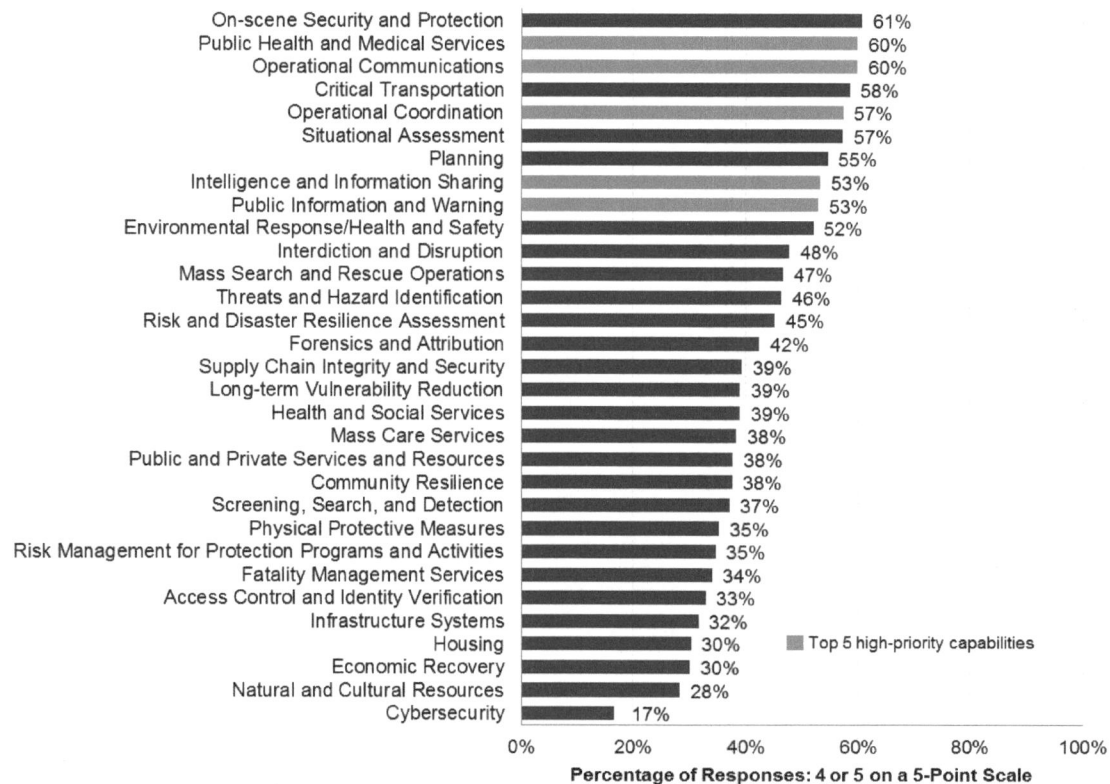

SPR Assessment of Current Capability

Capability	Percentage
On-scene Security and Protection	61%
Public Health and Medical Services	60%
Operational Communications	60%
Critical Transportation	58%
Operational Coordination	57%
Situational Assessment	57%
Planning	55%
Intelligence and Information Sharing	53%
Public Information and Warning	53%
Environmental Response/Health and Safety	52%
Interdiction and Disruption	48%
Mass Search and Rescue Operations	47%
Threats and Hazard Identification	46%
Risk and Disaster Resilience Assessment	45%
Forensics and Attribution	42%
Supply Chain Integrity and Security	39%
Long-term Vulnerability Reduction	39%
Health and Social Services	39%
Mass Care Services	38%
Public and Private Services and Resources	38%
Community Resilience	38%
Screening, Search, and Detection	37%
Physical Protective Measures	35%
Risk Management for Protection Programs and Activities	35%
Fatality Management Services	34%
Access Control and Identity Verification	33%
Infrastructure Systems	32%
Housing	30%
Economic Recovery	30%
Natural and Cultural Resources	28%
Cybersecurity	17%

■ Top 5 high-priority capabilities

Percentage of Responses: 4 or 5 on a 5-Point Scale

Figure 2: In the 2012 SPR, states and territories reported higher levels of performance for high-priority capabilities.

In addition to assessing each capability on a 5-point scale, states and territories also noted the relative importance of each capability by assigning it to one of three priority categories: high, medium, or low. Table 2 shows the five capabilities that states and territories rated most frequently as a high priority. Although some capabilities shifted slightly from their 2011 ranking, the broad prioritization remains consistent. All of the 2012 top-five high-priority capabilities fell within the 2011 top-ten rankings.

Table 2: High-priority capabilities in the 2012 SPR were among the highest rated capabilities.

Capability	Percentage of States and Territories Rating the Capability as "High Priority"
Operational Communications	92%
Public Health and Medical Services	90%
Intelligence and Information Sharing	90%
Public Information and Warning	88%
Operational Coordination	88%

Key finding: *In areas where current capability continues to lag, many states and territories do not expect to build additional capacity and intend to rely on Federal assets to close existing gaps.*

For each capability gap that the SPR identified, states and territories shared their observations on expected responsibilities for addressing that gap by selecting one of the four statements listed in Table 3. This response described states' and territories' expected activities to build necessary capability to meet the target they identified in their THIRAs, and may involve responsibilities for both the state and the Federal Government.

Table 3: Through the SPR, states and territories provided their views on expected responsibilities for addressing capability gaps.

Responsibility	Narrative Description
Entirely state	This capability target should be entirely attained by the jurisdiction; the jurisdiction will continue to increase this capability until the target is reached.
Mostly state	The jurisdiction will continue to increase this capability; some small portion of capacity will remain reliant on outside assets from higher levels of government.
Mostly Federal	The jurisdiction will potentially increase this capability; a significant portion of required capacity will remain reliant on outside assets from higher levels of government.
Entirely Federal	Current capability already represents the realistic maximum for the jurisdiction; the jurisdiction will continue to rely on outside assets from higher levels of government.

The results demonstrate that capabilities fall along a continuum that represents a gradual shift in perceived responsibility between state and Federal roles. At one extreme, 90 percent of respondents indicated that Situational Assessment and Planning are capabilities in which they expect the Federal Government to play the smallest role in addressing capability gaps. Conversely, over half of respondents reported a Federal role that exceeds state and territory responsibilities for five capabilities (Economic Recovery, Fatality Management Services, Cybersecurity, Forensics and Attribution, and Housing).

In general, states and territories reporting small capability gaps indicated that they intend to fill them by building capability themselves. However, when the capability gap was large, respondents typically suggested greater reliance on Federal support. Three capabilities (Access Control and Identity Verification, Risk Management for Protection Programs, and Physical Protective Measures) deviated from that trend, showing a limited Federal role, despite receiving relatively low capability ratings.

Figure 3 depicts these findings.[ii] These insights are based solely on state and territory observations as collected through the SPR. In a number of instances, these views may diverge from Federal perspectives on which level of government bears responsibility for addressing identified gaps. Regardless of whether consensus exists across levels of government, these observations on perceived responsibility among Federal and state partners are notable in an era of constrained budgets, as stakeholders prioritize action and seek cost-effective ways to address known gaps.

[ii] Bubble charts outlining these expected Federal and state roles to address identified gaps also appear in the individual narratives for each core capability. In some instances, the percentages displayed in these charts may total slightly more or less than 100 percent due to rounding.

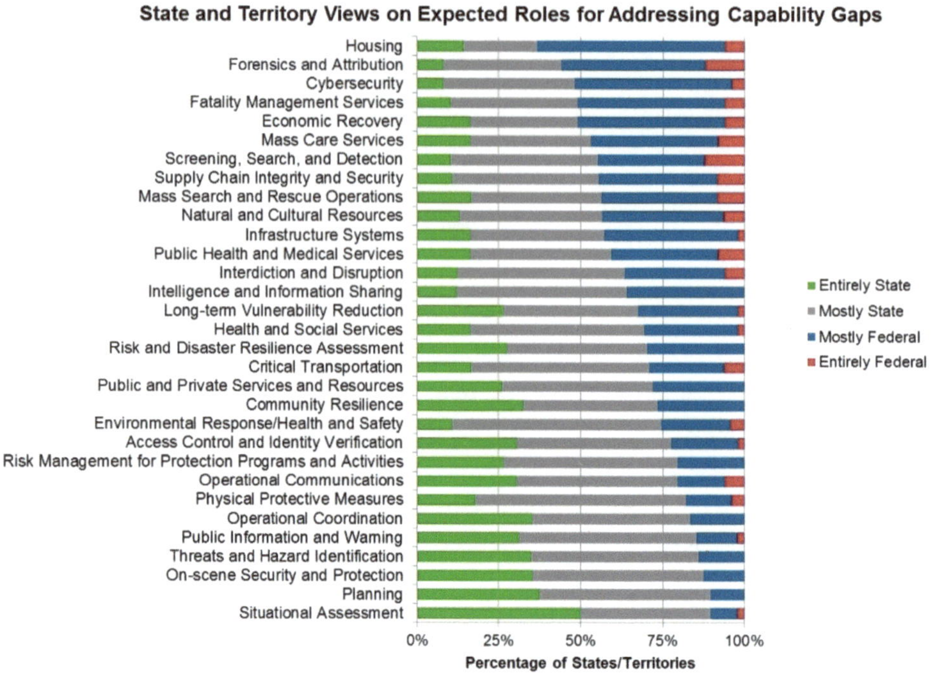

State and Territory Views on Expected Roles for Addressing Capability Gaps

Figure 3: SPR results illustrate state and territory perceptions about shared responsibility for addressing capability gaps.

Key finding: *Whole community partners continue to use preparedness assistance programs to maintain capability strengths and address identified gaps, while key Federal sponsors are identifying strategies to improve program effectiveness and efficiency.*

Preparedness grants continue to support implementation of the Goal through the development and sustainment of core capabilities across all mission areas. Numerous Federal agencies award preparedness-related grants, including DHS, USDA, the U.S. Department of Health and Human Services (HHS), the U.S. Department of Justice (DOJ), and the U.S. Department of Transportation (DOT). From FY 2010 to FY 2012, whole community partners invested approximately $7 billion in non-disaster preparedness funds through DHS programs (see Figure 4). Three-quarters of the funding was concentrated on a subset of core capabilities, including Physical Protective Measures, Long-Term

DHS Preparedness Grant Funding by Core Capability

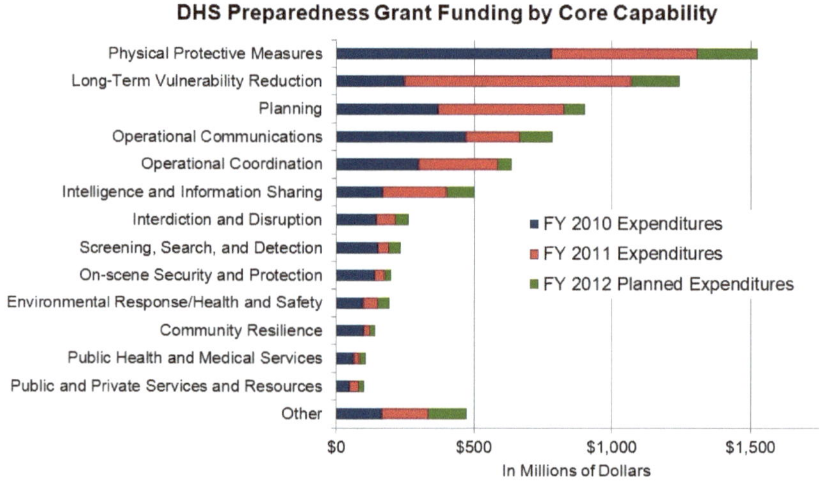

Figure 4: Six of the 31 core capabilities in the Goal account for 76 percent ($5.3 billion) of DHS's preparedness assistance from FY 2010 to FY 2012.

Vulnerability Reduction, and Planning. In FY 2012, DHS preparedness grants required grantees to belong to the Emergency Management Assistance Compact and to ensure that grant-funded capabilities are deployable outside of their community to support regional and national efforts. To improve overall grant program effectiveness, DHS continues to explore opportunities to streamline programs, improve the ability to measure performance, build readily deployable and shareable capabilities, and ensure that grant funds address capability gaps identified through THIRA and capability assessment processes. Together, these activities support implementation of the National Preparedness System.

HHS delivers preparedness assistance through the Assistant Secretary for Preparedness and Response (ASPR) Hospital Preparedness Program (HPP) and the Centers for Disease Control and Prevention (CDC) Public Health Emergency Preparedness (PHEP) program. HPP helps hospitals and other healthcare organizations build coalitions and strengthen medical surge capabilities, while PHEP supports preparedness activities in state and local public health departments. In 2011 and 2012, the HHS ASPR and CDC led a collaborative initiative to define essential public health and healthcare preparedness

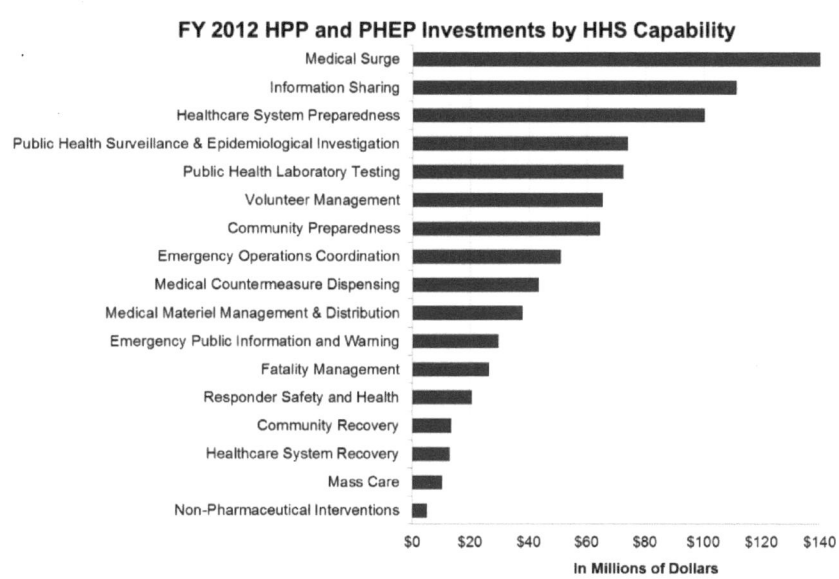

FY 2012 HPP and PHEP Investments by HHS Capability

Figure 5: Nearly $1 billion in HPP and PHEP preparedness assistance in FY 2012 supports investments across capabilities tailored to the health and medical communities.

capabilities and operationalize the public health and medical components of the core capabilities included in the Goal. Using these tailored capabilities, HPP and PHEP applicants were able to submit a single application for both cooperative agreements for the first time in May 2012. This program alignment fosters closer coordination among public health and healthcare system partners at all levels of government and improves efficiency in grant administration. Figure 5 shows the FY 2012 distribution of $352 million in HPP funding and of $619 million in PHEP funding across these tailored HHS capabilities.

Key finding: *Resilience initiatives are improving the Nation's ability to measure how well communities can prepare for and adapt to changing conditions, and withstand and recover rapidly from disruptions.*

Community resilience analysis considers economic, demographic, and societal factors that influence an entire community's capacity to adapt to changing conditions and withstand and rapidly recover from disruptions. For example, the Community and Regional Resilience Institute has developed the Community Resilience System, comprising web-based tools for communities to assess and improve their disaster resilience. Similarly, the University at Buffalo Regional Institute developed the Resilience Capacity Index, which uses 12 indicators across three broad categories—economic, socio-demographic, and community connectivity capacity—to assess community resilience for 361 metropolitan areas. Together, these and other tools are enhancing the Nation's ability to measure the resilience of entire communities to disaster.

As these evaluation techniques mature, additional studies of individual preparedness are prompting ideas for new approaches to community resilience that rely less on government sources and more on concerted whole community engagement. For example, FEMA's 2012 national survey on household preparedness revealed that nearly two-thirds of respondents had received disaster preparedness information within the past year from government, community, or media entities, with government being the source reported the least frequently. In terms of risk awareness, more participants reported believing that a natural disaster was likely to occur in their community. They also noted greater familiarity with the hazards that their communities face and with local alert and warning systems. Despite this greater awareness, national evaluations do not indicate progress in individual preparedness behaviors, such as building a disaster supplies kit and making a household emergency plan.

Common Core Capabilities

Planning

The Nation has well-established, mature planning capabilities that include strategic, operational, and tactical plans at all levels of government. The 2012 NPR identified Planning as an area of national strength, a trend that continues this year. The current NPR highlights ongoing attention to gaps in catastrophic planning, long-term recovery, and climate change adaptation.

Key finding: *FEMA Regions are prioritizing efforts to develop regional plans for all hazards, building upon previous regional catastrophic planning activities centered on region-specific threats and hazards.*

In September 2012, FEMA completed a new blueprint for regional planning activities for the next five years that prioritizes the development of plans addressing all hazards. This approach builds on experience from previous regional planning initiatives, which focused on specific regional threats and scenarios. One FEMA Region has completed its all-hazard plan and the other nine FEMA Regions are engaged in planning efforts. In addition, FEMA and its regional and state partners developed 30 hazard-specific regional catastrophic response plans between 2008 and 2012 (see Table 4). These plans increase the ability of all regional response partners to respond quickly and effectively to major disasters and to understand regional hazards, response capabilities, and planning assumptions. The hazards addressed in these regional catastrophic plans are generally among the hazards of concern that the FEMA Regions identified in their 2012 THIRAs.

Table 4: All 10 FEMA Regions (designated below as R1, R2, etc.) have partnered with states to develop 30 catastrophic plans that address relevant region-specific threats and hazards. (Note: Four regions have developed more than one plan for certain scenarios.)

Threats and Hazards in FEMA Regional Plans	R1	R2	R3	R4	R5	R6	R7	R8	R9	R10
CBRNE Response	•				•	•	•		•	
Earthquake or Tsunami	•	•		•	•	•	•	•	•	
Flooding or Dam Failure							•			
Hurricane or Typhoon	•	•		•		•			•	
Pandemic Influenza	•		•		•	•	•			•

Key finding: *The development and implementation of new Federal doctrine is strengthening whole community planning for long-term recovery. Similar Federal planning efforts are underway across other mission areas.*

New planning doctrine advanced national efforts to recover from disasters in 2012. Shortly after the release of the NDRF in September 2011, a national recovery tabletop exercise tested the application of the framework as part of NLE 2011. The exercise focused on an earthquake scenario in the New Madrid Seismic Zone and confirmed the importance of integrating the whole community into recovery planning. FEMA subsequently published a *Long-Term Community Recovery Toolbox* in March 2012, which provides tools and procedures to incorporate whole community partners into successful recovery efforts, including planning. Subsequently, in August 2012, a Senior Level Exercise featuring the NDRF examined challenges that senior Federal officials face when supporting recovery efforts after a multi-state disaster.

The NDRF and associated Recovery Support Functions have already guided recovery efforts for several events, including the 2011 Alabama tornadoes, the 2012 drought, and—most recently—Hurricanes Isaac and Sandy. The NDRF introduced the role of the FDRC, who serves as a focal point for recovery-based decision-making and coordination. Following Sandy, FDRCs deployed to New York and New Jersey to assess and address emerging challenges, including long-term housing needs and successful delivery of services and resources to eligible recipients.

The Federal Government is also finalizing three efforts to help unify emergency planning: National Planning Frameworks ("Frameworks") for the Prevention, Protection, Mitigation, and Response mission areas; Federal Interagency Operational Plans for each of the five mission areas; and a National Planning System to integrate planning across the whole community. Like the NDRF, the forthcoming Frameworks describe coordinating structures, identify roles and responsibilities, and align approaches across mission areas. The draft mission area operational plans build on the Frameworks by outlining the critical tasks and coordination mechanisms that Federal partners use to deliver core capabilities. The National Planning System focuses on the people, tools, processes, and coordination necessary for effective planning. Several National Planning System resources are under development, including a training program for planners, a stakeholder outreach tool, and a universal planning lexicon.

Key finding: *The Nation has made some progress in adaptation planning to address the long-term challenges posed by climate change and extreme weather, but planning for climate change remains an area of focus for preparedness activities nationally.*

In 2012, for the first time, Federal agencies included climate change adaptation plans in their sustainability plans for reducing greenhouse gas pollution, eliminating waste, and improving energy and water performance. These climate change plans outline initiatives to reduce the vulnerability of Federal programs, assets, and investments to the effects of climate change, including rising sea levels and extreme weather. At the state level, some adaptation efforts have also focused on planning initiatives; as of December 2012, at least 15 states had completed climate change adaptation plans.[2] Statewide adaptation strategies span a spectrum of activities, including research and education, as well as promoting policies that reduce vulnerability and strengthen resilience. Locally, adaptation efforts have included planning for land use; protecting infrastructure and ecosystems; regulating building, road, and bridge design and construction; and preparing for emergencies.[3] Despite these actions, the Government Accountability Office (GAO) cites climate change as a complex issue that poses significant financial risk to the Federal Government as a critical infrastructure owner and operator, an insurer, and contributor to disaster response and recovery efforts.

Preparedness Case Study: Improving School Safety Through Planning

In the wake of the December 2012 school shooting in Newtown, Connecticut, over 100 whole community leaders from across the country participated in a discussion about improving safety at schools, institutions of higher education, and houses of worship through emergency management plans. The White House-sponsored event took place in February 2013, and included three panels focused on the emergency management needs of these institutions, as well as on lessons learned from past mass shootings. Participants included experts in law enforcement, mental health, faith, education, and emergency management; survivors of gun violence; and senior officials from the U.S. Department of Education, DHS, and the FBI.

State and Territorial Preparedness Perspectives: Planning

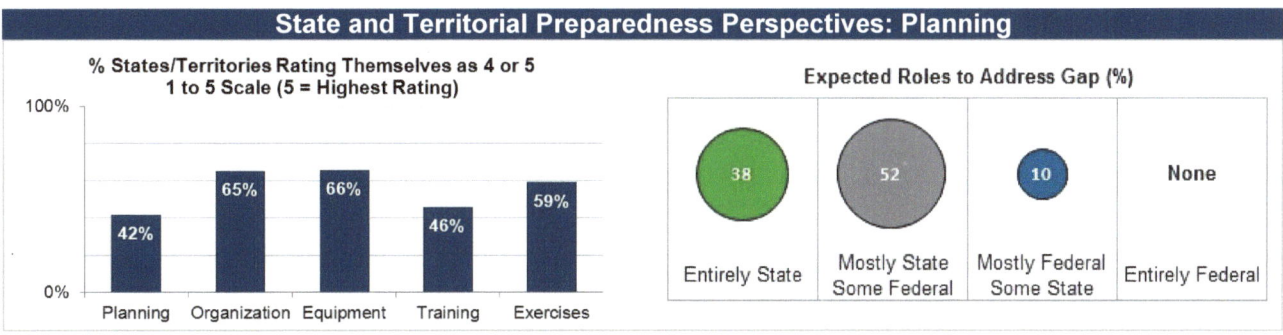

% States/Territories Rating Themselves as 4 or 5
1 to 5 Scale (5 = Highest Rating)

Planning 42% — Organization 65% — Equipment 66% — Training 46% — Exercises 59%

Expected Roles to Address Gap (%)

Entirely State 38 — Mostly State Some Federal 52 — Mostly Federal Some State 10 — Entirely Federal None

Public Information and Warning

The 2012 NPR focused on state confidence in public information and warning plans, as well as the coverage and accuracy of national warning systems, including the Integrated Public Alert and Warning System (IPAWS). The current NPR focuses on IPAWS implementation in 2012, with improved functionality via the Emergency Alert System and Wireless Emergency Alerts.

Key Finding: *Increases in IPAWS participation and capabilities improved the Nation's ability to alert individuals of imminent hazards. IPAWS improvements contributed to the development of Wireless Emergency Alerts (WEA) and a modernization of the Emergency Alert System (EAS) in 2012.*

IPAWS is a collection of approved standards and technologies for all emergency alert systems. These standards ensure that all alert delivery systems—from radio and television broadcasts to smartphones— can instantaneously distribute the same alert to affected populations. Federal, state, and local officials had access to IPAWS platforms 96.6 percent of the time in FY 2012, and FEMA is upgrading its data center and adding a backup server to increase operating availability in FY 2013. Individuals with disabilities and access and functional needs, as well as organizations representing these populations, also helped test and recommend improvements to the system. To facilitate IPAWS awareness, FEMA published the *State Toolkit for Adopting IPAWS* in March 2012. As of January 2013, FEMA approved 91 applications from state and local emergency management and response entities to generate and disseminate alerts through IPAWS, including 24 states and 13 major urban areas (see Figure 6).

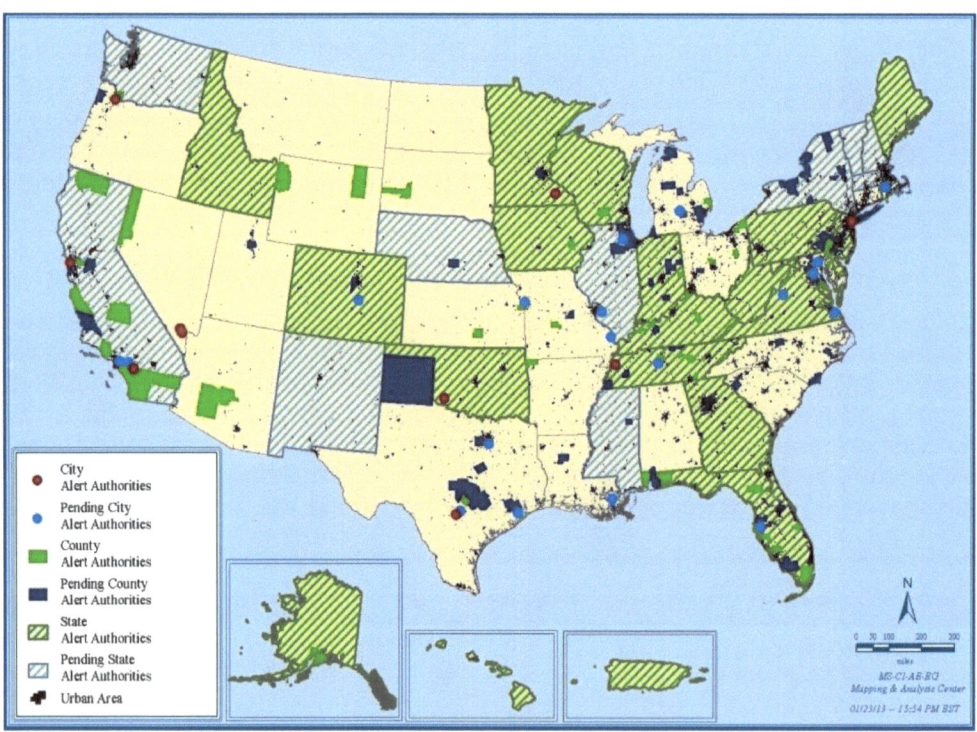

Figure 6: As of January 2013, FEMA had approved or processed over 200 applications for IPAWS authority.

In 2012, IPAWS enhancements contributed to implementation of WEA, which allow government officials to send geographically targeted wireless alerts to mobile telephones. WEA became fully operational in 2012 and are available to nearly 97 percent of all wireless telephone subscribers with compatible telephones.[4] Nearly all mobile telephones in the United States are expected to be compatible by 2014. In preparation for Sandy, New York City's Office of Emergency Management successfully issued WEA alerts, advising residents in the path of the storm to take shelter and advising those in flood-prone areas to evacuate. IPAWS has also improved the EAS, which requires participating radio, television, and cable service providers to broadcast Presidential addresses to the public. EAS participants broadcast AMBER, weather, and other emergency alerts on a voluntary basis. A November 2011 nationwide test of the EAS, which occurred prior to recent enhancements through IPAWS, identified technical areas for improvement, including device configuration. The Federal Communications Commission (FCC) subsequently required all EAS participants to be able to receive emergency alerts in the standard IPAWS format, decode the alerts, and broadcast them to the public by June 30, 2012.

Preparedness Case Study: Information Sharing via Twitter During Sandy

Amid the power outages after Sandy, millions turned to Twitter to share and receive information about the storm's impact. The Governors of New York and New Jersey—along with other government agencies, major corporations, nonprofit organizations, and the general public—used Twitter to communicate critical information. In the two-week period during and immediately following Sandy's landfall in New Jersey and New York, users sent more than 20 million Sandy-related Twitter posts, or "tweets," despite the loss of cellphone service during the peak of the storm. Approximately one-third of these tweets involved media and government posts, eyewitness accounts, or users "re-tweeting" this information within their own networks. One-quarter of the tweets featured photos and videos from users.

State and Territorial Preparedness Perspectives: Public Information and Warning

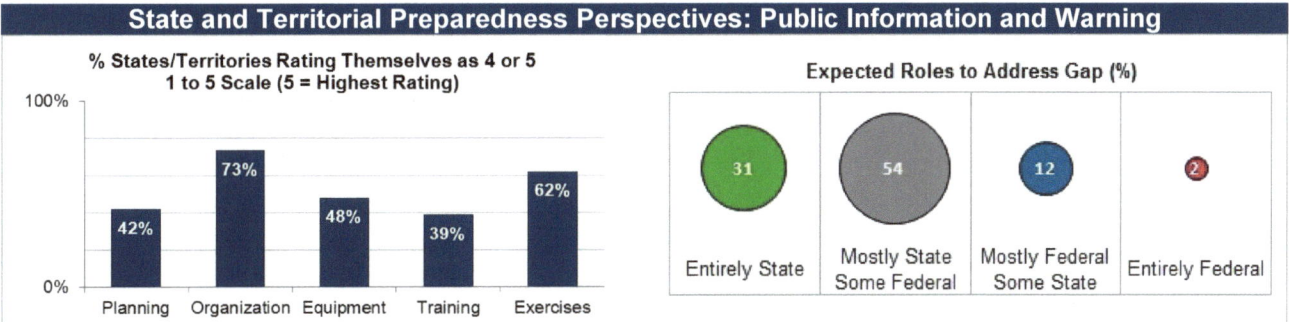

Operational Coordination

The Nation sustained progress in standardizing incident management approaches and creating new coordination mechanisms to address specific threats and hazards. The 2012 NPR highlighted operational coordination mechanisms in the Response mission area. Accomplishments this year include operational coordination achievements in the Prevention and Protection mission areas with international partners and among state and Federal military personnel. In addition, 34 percent of states and territories reported making the most progress in Operational Coordination in the past year, more than in any other core capability.

Key Finding: *The Nation has forged international partnerships to improve operational coordination in law enforcement, cargo security, and passenger screening.*

In April 2012, the United States and the European Union (EU) concluded an agreement on the use and transfer of passenger name records that air carriers flying between the EU and the United States are required to provide to DHS. In 2012, the United States also completed arrangements formalizing mutual recognition of port security inspection regimes with the European Commission and of "trusted traveler" programs with Australia and South Korea. The United States finalized arrangements establishing air cargo security reciprocity with Canada, Switzerland, and the EU, and developed a joint cargo security strategy with Canada to harmonize maritime cargo screening.

As part of the International Port Security Program, the U.S. Coast Guard (USCG) removed conditions of entry requirements on vessels arriving from the Republic of Congo and Indonesia in 2011 and 2012, respectively, determining that port security in those countries had improved to international standards. Furthermore, in 2012, the United States and Canada announced the first two locations of the Integrated Cross-Border Maritime Law Enforcement Operations program, also known as Shiprider. Through this program, U.S. and Canadian law enforcement personnel conduct joint patrols on vessels on or near the maritime border to better integrate their operations and combat cross-border illegal activity. In FY 2012, the United States and Canada also conducted 50 joint law enforcement operations along the northern border, significantly exceeding the planned annual target of 12 operations.

Key Finding: *Continued progress implementing the dual-status commander concept helps to promote unity of effort between the operational activities of state and Federal military personnel in response to domestic incidents and in preparation for major special events.*

The concept of the dual-status commander allows a single commander—either a Federal active duty officer or a National Guard officer—to exercise command and control over Federal military personnel and non-federalized National Guard military personnel through separate Federal and state chains of command during disasters and major special events, including National Special Security Events. In June 2012, the U.S. Department of Defense (DOD) issued a concept of operations establishing designation criteria and training requirements for dual-status commanders. As of June 2012, 54 states and territories have trained and certified at least one officer to serve as a dual-status commander; 37 states and territories have trained and certified at least two officers. In 2012, dual-status commanders supported the North Atlantic Treaty Organization Summit in Chicago; the Republican National Convention in Tampa, Florida; the Democratic National Convention in Charlotte, North Carolina; and responses to wildfires in California and Colorado and to Hurricanes Isaac and Sandy.

Preparedness Case Study: Emergency Management Assistance Compact (EMAC) Member Responses to Sandy

EMAC enables its members (i.e., all 50 states, the District of Columbia, Puerto Rico, Guam, and the U.S. Virgin Islands) to offer mutual assistance quickly during governor-declared states of emergency, using pre-existing resource typing, reimbursement, communication, and personnel-credentialing systems. A National EMAC Liaison Team maintains a presence in FEMA's National Response Coordination Center to coordinate assistance. In FY 2011, 39 states conducted a total of 80 exercises that incorporated EMAC. In addition, 39 states provided 334 EMAC training opportunities to non-emergency management personnel. This training paid dividends in the response to and recovery from Sandy. As of November 2012, more than 2,400 civilian and National Guard personnel from 35 states deployed to affected areas through EMAC.

State and Territorial Preparedness Perspectives: Operational Coordination

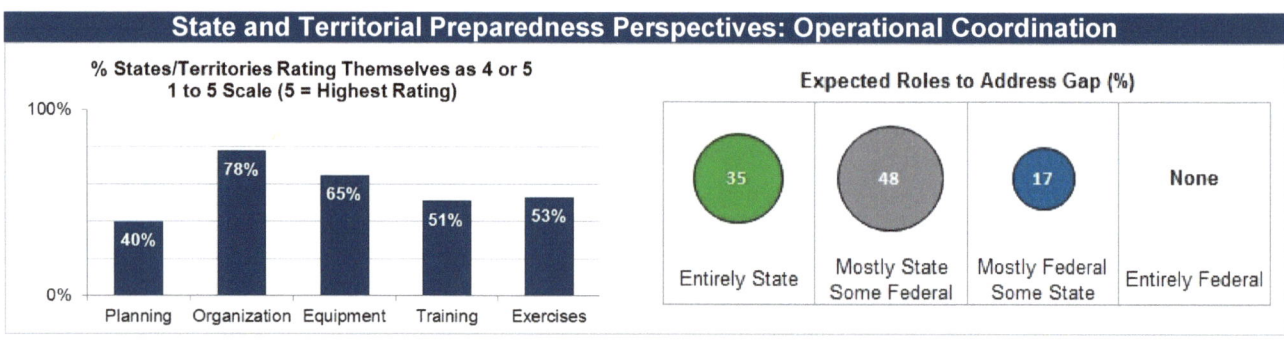

% States/Territories Rating Themselves as 4 or 5
1 to 5 Scale (5 = Highest Rating)

Planning	Organization	Equipment	Training	Exercises
40%	78%	65%	51%	53%

Expected Roles to Address Gap (%)

Entirely State	Mostly State Some Federal	Mostly Federal Some State	Entirely Federal
35	48	17	None

Prevention Core Capabilities

Forensics and Attribution

The 2012 NPR noted that terrorism-prevention capabilities focused on forensics analysis and attribution reside almost entirely with Federal agencies, a trend that continued this year. The 2012 SPR results showed that 56 percent of states and territories are mostly or wholly reliant on the Federal Government to close Forensics and Attribution capability gaps. Current NPR findings explore growing national capabilities for sharing biometric data and processing digital evidence through regional computer forensics laboratories.

Key Finding: *Federal agencies are improving biometric data sharing by updating and adding technologies that assist in the capture, storage, and exchange of biometric data.*

Biometric data are measurable biological or behavioral characteristics used to identify an individual, such as fingerprints, deoxyribonucleic acid (DNA), iris scans, and other unique characteristics. These data help prevent future terrorist acts against the United States by enabling Federal, state, local, tribal, and territorial law enforcement officials to rapidly identify individuals and conduct investigations of known or suspected terrorists and criminals. The ability to share and access this information—consistent with applicable laws and standards regarding privacy and civil liberties protections—is critical for law enforcement activities at all levels to prevent terrorism. The Federal Government is improving the ability of authorized users to access this data quickly. For example, DHS reported that the average time to conduct searches of biometric watch-list data from U.S. ports of entry and U.S. consulates was less than one minute.

US-VISIT is a key provider of identification and analysis services based on biometric and biographical information. Each day, 30,000 authorized Federal, state and local government users query data from this DHS program. US-VISIT supplies the technology for collecting and storing biometric data, provides analysis of the data to decision-makers, and ensures data integrity. The volume of data requests through US-VISIT's two automated identification systems—the Automated Biometric Identification System (IDENT) and the Arrival and Departure Information System (ADIS)—continues to grow. Currently, the IDENT system processes approximately 240,000 transactions per day, with an average response time under 10 seconds, and the ADIS system is adding between 13 and 14 million records annually.

The FBI Next Generation Identification (NGI) program is gradually replacing the Integrated Automated Fingerprint Identification System, which contains fingerprints, mug shots, and criminal histories. The NGI provides more comprehensive information on an individual's criminal history, physical features, and other biometric data. The NGI plans include palm print–recognition capabilities, as well as identification of facial features, bodily scars, tattoos, and other unique markings. Transition from the Integrated Automated Fingerprint Identification System to the NGI improved accuracy in fingerprint searches from 92 percent to over 99 percent by 2012. The NGI's Repository for Individuals of Special Concern (RISC) Rapid Search launched in 2011. It is accessible to local law enforcement officers through a mobile device and enables searches across over 1.2 million fingerprints instantly. The RISC Rapid Search system processes over 500 transactions per day, with a response time of less than seven seconds.

Key Finding: *Federal resources for computer forensics are strategically located across the Nation to support Federal, state, and local law enforcement by processing digital evidence for criminal and counterterrorism investigations.*

Digital evidence has become part of nearly every criminal and counterterrorism investigation. The ability to process these data, however, can be costly and often exceeds the capacity of individual Federal, state, and local law enforcement agencies. To address this need, 16 FBI-sponsored Regional Computer Forensics Laboratories rapidly process digital evidence to support law enforcement investigations. Each facility is a full-service forensic laboratory with trained analysts who can process digital evidence from cell phones, computers, and other electronic storage devices. These regional laboratories have become a critical asset supporting Federal, state, and local law enforcement investigations, and are broadening their capabilities to meet growing demand. From 2009 to 2011, requests for assistance from Regional

Computer Forensics Laboratories increased from 5,616 to 6,318; the number of terabytes processed nearly doubled from 2,334 to 4,263; and the number of digital forensics examinations rose from 6,016 to 7,629 (see Figure 7). Additionally, these resources have played key roles in recent counterterrorism investigations. For example, in 2011, the Kentucky Regional Computer Forensics Laboratory supported the investigation of two Iraqi nationals conspiring to purchase weapons and ship them to Al-Qaeda in Iraq.

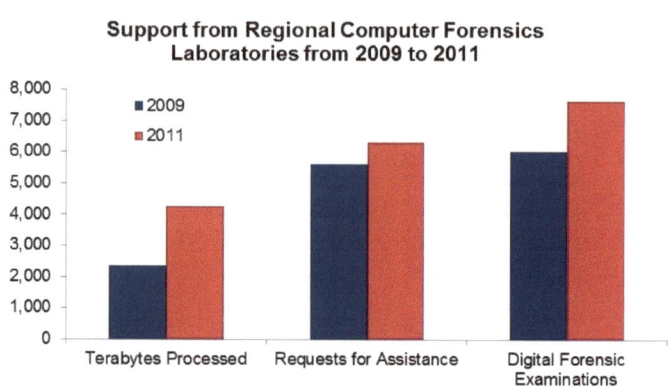

Support from Regional Computer Forensics Laboratories from 2009 to 2011

Figure 7: Demand for specialized capabilities to process evidence from the FBI's Regional Computer Forensics Laboratories has increased steadily since 2009.

In addition to the regional FBI laboratories, USSS Cyber Electronic Crimes Task Forces continue to bring together law enforcement, academia, and private-sector stakeholders to confront and suppress technology-based criminal activity. The 31 task forces consist of 2,700 Federal, state, local and international law enforcement members; 3,100 private-sector partners; and 300 members of academia. The USSS has 180 computer forensics agents assigned to the task forces nationally to support cyber incident response efforts and forensic examination of digital evidence. From 2009 to 2011, the task forces more than doubled the number of forensic examinations annually (from 3,281 to 8,688) and quadrupled the number of terabytes processed (from 265 to 1,090).

Preparedness Case Study: USSS Training in Mobile Device Forensics

In 2008, USSS launched the Cell Phone Forensic Facility at the University of Tulsa. This facility conducts research in mobile device forensics and evidence collection to help counter a surge in criminal use of digital technology and the nearly 400-percent increase in smart phone malware since 2010. The facility also offers specialized training for USSS field agents in the Electronic Crimes Special Agent Program. In 2012, field agents who had trained at the Tulsa facility examined over 1,400 digital devices.

State and Territorial Preparedness Perspectives: Forensics and Attribution

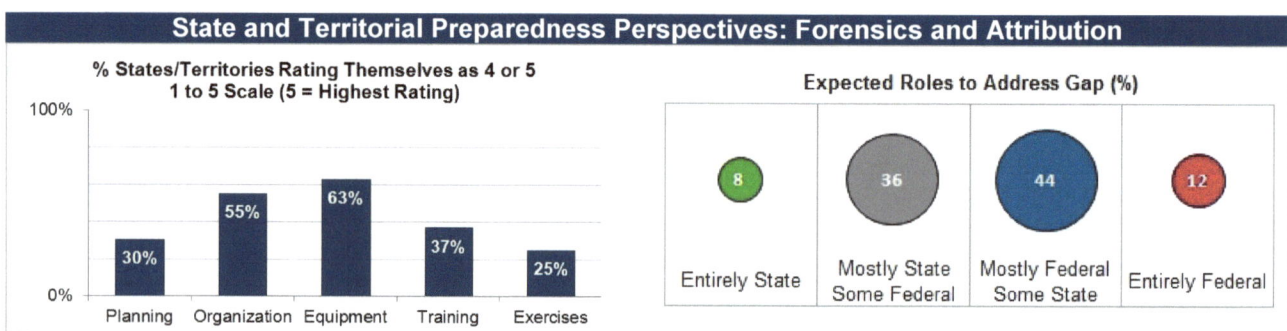

Prevention/Protection Core Capabilities

Intelligence and Information Sharing

Intelligence and information sharing partners across all levels of government continue to collaborate to enhance sharing capabilities. New national strategies and Federal governance bodies also guide the development of common and consistent policies to support fusion centers. Current NPR findings highlight the continued maturation of the national network of fusion centers since 2011.

Key Finding: *The National Network of Fusion Centers demonstrated continued progress in enhancing critical operational capabilities, as evaluated through an annual performance assessment.*

In accordance with national strategies and policy, the Federal Government has formalized processes for guiding support to fusion centers and evaluating their capabilities. In particular, DHS, in collaboration with fusion center directors and Federal interagency partners, has instituted a repeatable annual assessment process to measure the progress made by the national network of fusion centers in maturing state and local intelligence processes and analytic capabilities. This assessment aims to objectively evaluate fusion centers and the national network as a whole in supporting information sharing, while simultaneously providing valuable feedback on support from the Federal Government to mature and sustain the network.

As of 2012, the national network made significant progress in developing approved plans, policies, and standard operating procedures to codify their business processes. For example, all 77 designated fusion centers have approved privacy, civil rights, and civil liberties policies. In addition, more than 92 percent of fusion centers have documented and approved plans, policies, or standard operating procedures for four identified critical operational capabilities: receive, analyze, disseminate, and gather. Progress has increased steadily since 2010, as detailed in Figure 8. As of 2012, 97 percent of fusion centers identified counterterrorism as a core mission focus. Additionally, 96 percent indicate that they are engaged in an all-crimes approach, and 70 percent

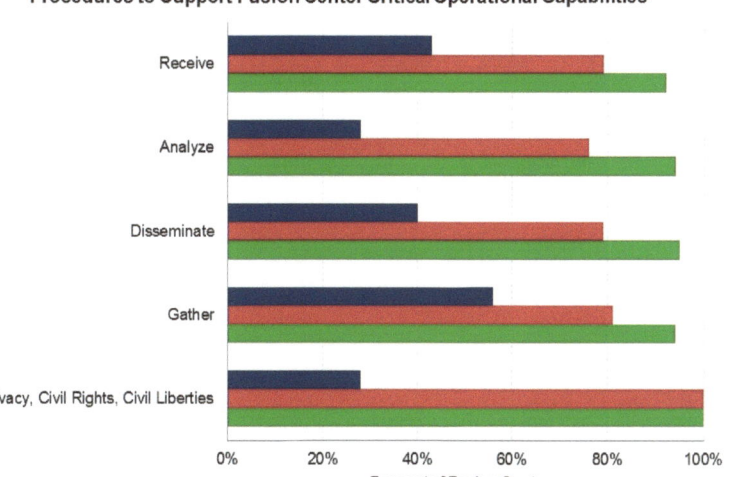

Progress in Establishing Plans, Policies, and Standard Operating Procedures to Support Fusion Center Critical Operational Capabilities

Figure 8: Annual capabilities and performance assessments show steady progress across all critical operational capabilities for fusion centers.

indicate they are applying an all-hazards approach. The 2012 SPR confirmed state and territory advances in Intelligence and Information Sharing. Ninety percent of states and territories identified this capability as a high priority, and nearly one-quarter reported making the most progress in this capability in the past year.

DHS also established a maturity model for the national network of fusion centers as part of the assessment program. This model identifies four stages—fundamental, emerging, enhanced, and mature—through which the national network will progress as it moves towards full capability and operational integration as a unified system. As of February 2013, the national network is in the second stage of the maturity model, with ongoing efforts to build and achieve full capacity.

Key Finding: *Nationwide training on suspicious activity reporting is strengthening the ability of partners across all levels of government to identify and share relevant information to prevent crimes and terrorism activity.*

The Nationwide Suspicious Activity Reporting Initiative (NSI) Program Management Office partners with personnel from the FBI, DHS, fusion centers, law enforcement, and homeland security to enhance information sharing on suspicious activities, while protecting privacy, civil rights, and civil liberties. By 2012, over 288,000 law enforcement officers had received training to recognize behavior and incidents that may indicate criminal activity associated with terrorism. An additional 51,000 preparedness and security partners—including emergency managers, fire personnel, emergency medical services (EMS) personnel, probation and parole officers, public safety communications, and private-sector security personnel—had also completed new awareness training on their roles in the process. Together, these resources enable critical partners to share timely suspicious activity report information with the FBI for investigation, and with fusion centers and FBI Field Intelligence Groups for analysis. As of 2012, analysts nationwide have searched the NSI Federated Search database almost 70,000 times, accessing more than 25,000 suspicious activity reports. From 2010 to 2012, access to these reports through the FBI's eGuardian system led to over 1,300 investigations.

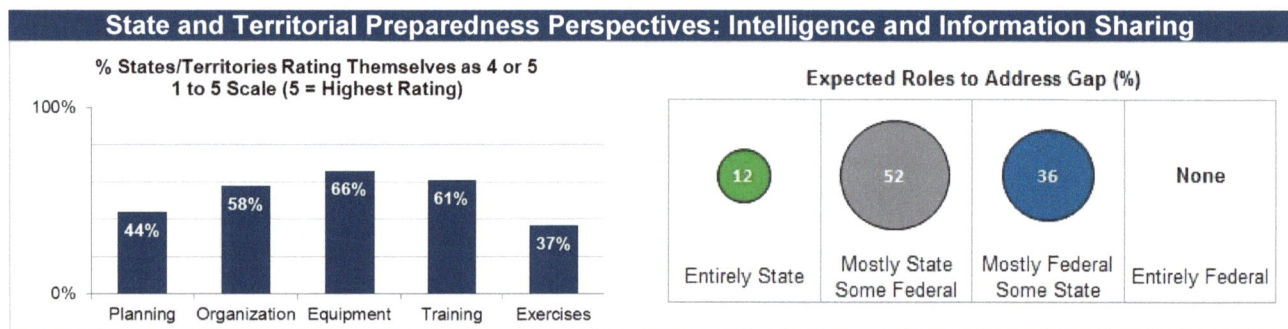

Interdiction and Disruption

The 2012 NPR outlined Federal, state, and local assets and resources available to interdict and disrupt terrorist threats, as well as the training and exercises designed to support these resources. Current NPR findings show continued progress in training for security partners, and describe additional capabilities for identifying and intercepting terrorism-related financial transactions. In particular, nearly one-quarter of states and territories indicated making the most progress in developing Interdiction and Disruption capabilities in the past year.

Key Finding: *Federal agencies are meeting increased demand from law enforcement for financial intelligence and investigative support.*

Federal agencies have developed advanced capabilities for identifying illegal financial transactions that may be linked to terrorists or terrorist activities. The FBI Terrorism Financing Operations Section operates out of all 56 FBI field offices, and supports counterterrorism investigations by analyzing financial intelligence and pursuing credible leads. Since 2010, the Terrorism Financing Operations Section has assisted law enforcement investigations of individuals channeling money from the United States to terrorist organizations in Pakistan, Lebanon, and the Arabian Peninsula.

Federal agencies also support law enforcement investigations of illegal financial transactions across all levels of government. For example, the U.S. Department of

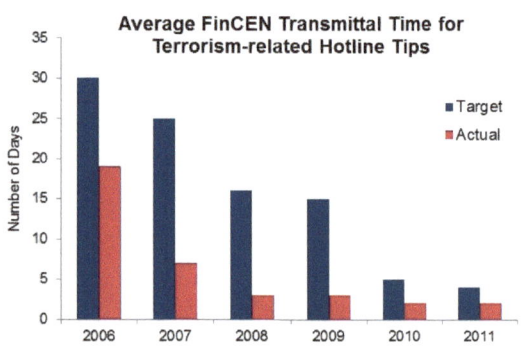

Figure 9: Since 2006, FinCEN has exceeded performance targets for transmitting terrorism-related hotline tips.

the Treasury's Financial Crimes Enforcement Network (FinCEN) supports investigations, monitors trends, and works with other Federal and international security partners to prevent acts of terrorism. FinCEN has reduced the average transmittal time for terrorism-related hotline tips from 19 days in 2006 to just 2 days in 2011, as outlined in Figure 9. FinCEN also provides a mechanism for law enforcement agencies to communicate with financial institutions during investigations through the Secure Information Sharing System. As of 2011, law enforcement agencies and other FinCEN customers issued over 1,500 total requests for information on financial transactions, with 378 of these requests directly related to terrorism.

Key Finding: *Federal agencies continue to provide training for security partners in chemical, biological, radiological, nuclear, and explosive (CBRNE) interdiction.*

The Federal Government maintains a commitment to train personnel and security partners in CBRNE interdiction. For example, since the start of 2011, the USCG trained over 6,000 of its personnel in CBRNE detection and response. The FBI's Hazardous Devices School trains state and local law enforcement to locate, identify, render safe, and dispose of improvised hazardous devices. In 2011, students at the Hazardous Devices School completed 2,295 weeks of instruction. In addition, DHS's Office for Bombing Prevention provided improvised explosive device prevention and protection instruction to more than 6,300 security partners in 2012, and added more than 2,400 users to its Technical Resource for Incident Prevention (TRIPwire) information-sharing platform. FEMA's National Domestic Preparedness Consortium and the Center for Domestic Preparedness also continued specialized training to prepare first responders for CBRNE events, training approximately 95,000 students from 2011 to 2012. Moreover, the U.S. Department of Energy's (DOE's) Federal Radiological Monitoring and Assessment Center and DOD's Defense Threat Reduction University provide training to federal, state, and local agencies to enhance capabilities for managing CBRNE events. Finally, Federal agencies also deliver joint technical assistance and other support to local jurisdictions to strengthen prevention and protection planning capabilities. For example, the Joint Counterterrorism and Awareness Workshop Series and Multi-Jurisdiction Improvised Explosive Device Security Planning are cooperative efforts that include the National Counterterrorism Center, DHS, and the FBI, and they help local jurisdictions prepare for coordinated terrorist attacks through collaborative planning.

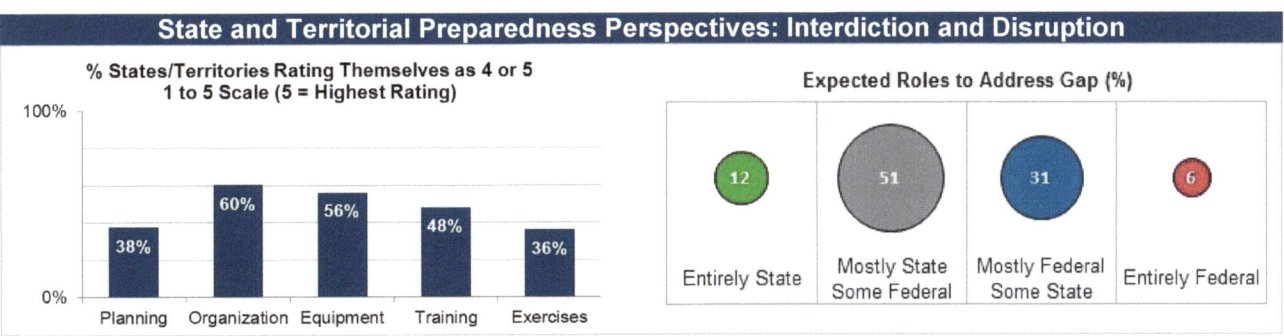

Screening, Search, and Detection

The Nation continues to maintain the CBRNE screening and detection capabilities outlined in the 2012 NPR. Current NPR findings explore the growing maturity of these resources, including air domain screening; implementation of the Global Nuclear Detection Architecture; and biosurveillance strategies, tools, and programs that engage state, local, tribal, and territorial partners.

Key Finding: *The Transportation Security Administration (TSA) and partner agencies are improving the efficiency and effectiveness of passenger, baggage, and air cargo screening.*

Screening passengers and baggage is critical for the Nation's overall ability to prevent acts of terrorism. During 2012, DHS screened nearly 1 billion individuals and examined more than 12 million inbound cargo containers at ports to support prevention activities nationally. TSA screens 100 percent of checked and carry-on baggage for dangerous items, including explosives. TSA and partner agencies are also providing enhanced security for the traveling public by strengthening terrorism watch-lists. Of all travelers flying within, to, or from the United States, 100 percent are screened against terrorism watch-lists before they receive boarding passes. The U.S. Department of State is working with international partners to ensure that these watch-lists reflect the latest information on known or suspected terrorists.

The 9/11 Commission Act of 2007 mandated that DHS also establish a system to screen 100 percent of air cargo transported on all passenger aircraft by the end of 2010. In December 2012, TSA met that target for the first time for inbound air cargo on flights originating outside the United States. To achieve this goal, the United States relied on partnerships with international stakeholders, including arrangements from 2012 with the EU, Switzerland, and Canada to establish cargo security reciprocity.

Key Finding: *Biosurveillance strategies and monitoring systems facilitate communication and coordination among Federal, state, local, tribal, and territorial public health partners.*

Issued in July 2012, the *National Strategy for Biosurveillance* integrates Federal biosurveillance efforts to understand threats and improve coordination. The strategy outlines a coordinated approach involving Federal, state, local, territorial, and tribal governments; the private sector; non-governmental organizations; and international partners. As part of this initiative, the National Biosurveillance Integration System links biosurveillance programs across the United States. In 2012, the system reported 15-hour operational response times to biosurveillance queries, exceeding the performance target of 48 hours or less.

National biosurveillance efforts also rely on collaboration with state, local, tribal, and territorial agencies. The DHS-managed BioWatch program is one of the Nation's federally managed and locally operated monitoring and detection systems designed to identify releases of aerosolized biological threat agents in more than 30 metropolitan areas. As of 2012, 14 BioWatch jurisdictional coordinators work closely with local, state, and regional planning teams in the field to advise public health, emergency management, and other local officials on BioWatch operations. Similarly, CDC's BioSense program employs a collaborative approach to create a cohesive and responsive syndromic surveillance system. Using emergency department data gathered from state and local health departments into a cloud-based environment, BioSense continuously monitors the public health system to improve emergency response to threats at the local, state, and national levels. In 2012, CDC launched a redesigned version of BioSense and achieved the goal of adding 24 health departments to the program.

Coordination across all levels of government is also essential to protecting the Nation's food and agricultural systems. For example, FoodSHIELD is a web-based portal that facilitates communication and coordination among Federal, state, and local entities responsible for protecting this critical infrastructure. Managed by the National Center for Food Protection and Defense, FoodSHIELD reported 3,500 users as of 2012, with representation from all 50 states, as well as Federal and international partners. In addition, the DHS Office of Health Affairs is collaborating to support the food and agriculture sector, including a recently updated template for food emergency response planning and ongoing efforts to develop uniform training curricula on emergency planning for response to animal disease outbreaks.

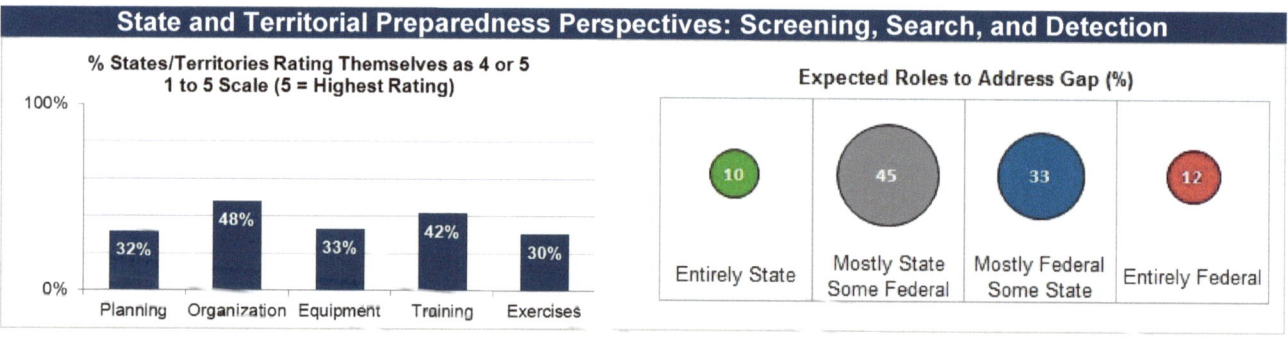

Protection Core Capabilities

Access Control and Identity Verification

The 2012 NPR noted the progress that Federal agencies and owners and operators of critical facilities have made in using standardized credentials and background checks to control admittance to secure locations and systems. Current NPR findings explore the progress made at the Federal level in requiring smartcard use to access critical networks and to achieve credential system interoperability at all levels of government.

Key Finding: *Federal agencies continue to make progress issuing Personal Identity Verification (PIV) smartcards that meet Homeland Security Presidential Directive (HSPD) 12 standards, with growing emphasis on requiring employee smartcards for access to information systems.*

Standardized smartcards help the Federal Government verify employee and contractor identities and control access to physical locations and information networks. Since 2011, Federal agencies have continued substantial progress in issuing PIV smartcards to Federal employees and contractors, as required by HSPD-12 (see Figure 10). As of September 2012, agencies reported that 96 percent of Federal employees and contractors requiring smartcards had received them, an increase of 7 percent over the previous year. Several agencies cited challenges issuing cards to personnel in remote field office locations and to seasonal or temporary employees.

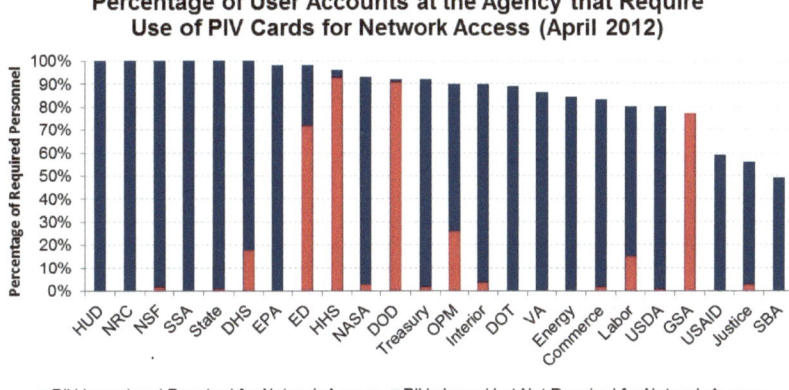

Figure 10: As of April 2012, over 95 percent of the Federal workforce possessed PIV cards, in compliance with standards adopted under HSPD-12.

For instance, the Small Business Administration has issued cards to more than 90 percent of its permanent workforce, but the agency relies on a large reserve workforce for disaster assistance.

Federal agencies are also making some progress implementing information systems that require the use of smartcards for access. A FY 2011 Office of Management and Budget report revealed that only eight agencies required the use of smartcards by any of their employees to access agency information networks. By April 2012, the number increased to 15 agencies, with a reported 56 percent of all Federal user accounts requiring smartcards for network access.

Key Finding: *Most state, local, tribal, and territorial governments have not adopted interoperable access control and credentialing systems based on Federal standards. However, ongoing efforts by Federal agencies and whole community partners are aimed at providing common frameworks and reducing barriers to adoption by non-Federal entities.*

A national interoperable credentialing system—a system where a common set of requirements and processes are used to develop identification credentials across different jurisdictions and organizations— aids the timely provision of goods and services during disasters and helps protect critical infrastructure and information systems. For example, when mutual aid is required, responders from outside jurisdictions with interoperable credentials often receive quicker access to incident sites than others. In 2009, the Federal Chief Information Officers Council released guidance that defined the Personal Identity Verification Interoperability (PIV-I) standard to help non-Federal entities establish interoperable credentialing systems. However, as of 2012, fewer than 20 non-Federal jurisdictions had adopted or were in the process of adopting credentialing systems consistent with the guidance. In fall 2012, Sandy reinforced the need for these systems to ensure the access of key personnel to damaged areas to support response and recovery operations.

Many jurisdictions face challenges in adopting interoperable credentialing and access control systems, including difficulties replacing legacy systems, sustaining funding, ensuring alignment with Federal efforts, and demonstrating value to stakeholders. These challenges are evident in the 2012 SPR results, in which Access Control and Identity Verification is rated among the weakest, falling within the bottom 25 percent of all capabilities. However, emergency response stakeholders are working to address these issues through various working groups. In 2012, the Emergency Services Sector Coordinating Council Credentialing and Disaster Reentry Working Group published a joint standard operating procedure template to guide state and local jurisdictions in developing protocols for interoperable access control following a disaster. The new template reflected lessons learned from exercises sponsored by InfraGard in 2009 and 2010, in which several Gulf Coast states tested early prototypes of the procedure. It also helps address planning challenges identified in the 2012 SPR.

Preparedness Case Study: Interoperable Credentials for Healthcare Officials

In 2008, the Southwest Texas Regional Advisory Council—a regional council in the Texas Trauma/Emergency Healthcare System representing 53 hospitals and 70 EMS agencies—launched a new identification system that included interoperable smart credentials. By April 2012, the Council had issued more than 3,000 federally interoperable credentials that were consistent with the PIV-I standard. Physicians received the credentials to access hospitals, offices, pharmacies, labs, parking garages, and secure areas in certain buildings. The region can now deploy handheld authentication devices to validate the identity of local, state, and Federal personnel arriving on-scene at an incident.

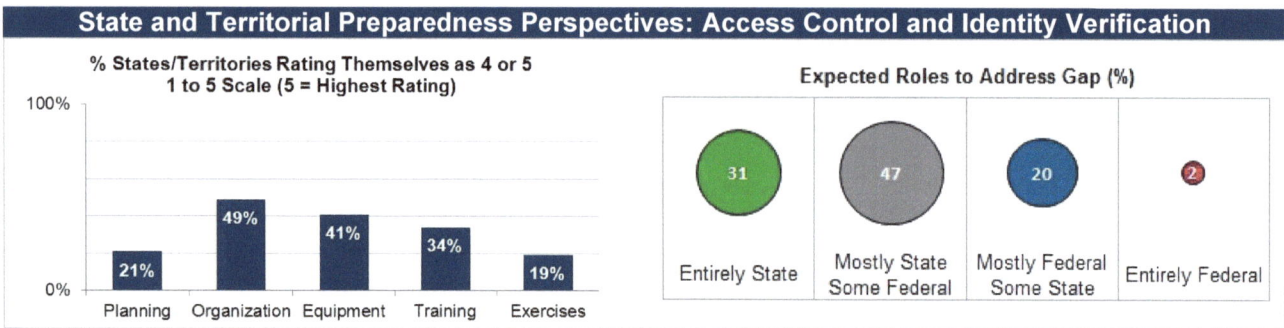

State and Territorial Preparedness Perspectives: Access Control and Identity Verification

% States/Territories Rating Themselves as 4 or 5
1 to 5 Scale (5 = Highest Rating)

Planning: 21%
Organization: 49%
Equipment: 41%
Training: 34%
Exercises: 19%

Expected Roles to Address Gap (%)

Entirely State: 31
Mostly State Some Federal: 47
Mostly Federal Some State: 20
Entirely Federal: 2

Cybersecurity

The 2012 NPR highlighted Cybersecurity as an area for improvement, noting that relevant stakeholders expanded efforts to address the growing threat to critical infrastructure and systems, but faced challenges in understanding cyber risk. Current NPR findings show that cyber efforts have matured over the past year, but work remains in this complex capability, including increasing state cyber capabilities and developing a cyber workforce.

Key Finding: *A combination of planning initiatives, exercises, and real-world events increased the ability of the Federal Government and the private sector to work together and respond effectively to cyber incidents.*

Years of experience with physical disasters led the Federal Government and partners to develop a suite of response doctrine, plans, and policies. Until recently, equivalent guidance did not exist to address cyber-related threats. To begin addressing this gap, in 2010, the Federal Government developed a draft *National Cyber Incident Response Plan* (NCIRP), which establishes an operational response structure for significant cyber incidents.

NLE 2012 tested the draft NCIRP and examined the Nation's capabilities pertaining to a significant cyber event or a series of events. Over 60 organizations participated in NLE 2012, including Federal agencies, state and territorial governments, international partners, and private-sector/non-governmental organizations. The exercise allowed stakeholders to identify gaps—such as the need for common terminology and pre-defined agreements for support during response—that impede a coordinated national response to cyber-related threats. NLE 2012 also helped clarify how the Federal Government can use existing legal authorities and coordination structures when responding to a cyber incident. In response, DHS plans to update the draft NCIRP to address challenges identified in NLE 2012. In addition, the National Cybersecurity and Communications Integration Center (NCCIC) started developing a series of capability-based cyber incident action plans to complement the draft NCIRP and to improve operational coordination with other government and industry partners.

As a sector-specific example, in May 2012, DOE released the Electricity Subsector Cybersecurity Risk Management Process, developed in collaboration with the National Institute of Standards and Technology (NIST) and the North American Electric Reliability Corporation. The guideline helps utilities understand their cybersecurity risks, assess severity, and allocate resources more efficiently, regardless of the organization's size or governance structure.

Lessons learned from NLE 2012 and other interagency efforts have helped increase coordination between the government and the private sector, although work remains to enhance Cybersecurity capabilities nationally. To help address this priority, in February 2013, the President issued an Executive Order on critical infrastructure cybersecurity, which outlines key initiatives for Federal implementation within the next year. The new policy calls for expanded partnerships with critical infrastructure owners and operators to improve cybersecurity information sharing and to develop and implement a cybersecurity framework to address cyber risk.

Key Finding: *DHS and DOD—including the National Security Agency (NSA) —are establishing new recruitment, training, and retention policies and programs to expand the expertise of the Federal cyber workforce.*

In 2009, a collaborative effort between DHS, the Office of Personnel Management, and the Office of Management and Budget resulted additional authorities for DHS to hire individuals with critical cyber skills over the next three years. In June 2012, DHS announced the formation of a Task Force on CyberSkills to identify ways to foster a national cybersecurity workforce and address personnel deficits. The task force's fall 2012 report defined mission-critical cybersecurity skills and set a near-term goal of hiring 600 DHS employees with those skills. Implementation of these recommendations is underway. Alongside DHS, DOD, including the NSA, has continued efforts to increase the pipeline of cybersecurity professionals in the Federal workforce, running cyber "boot camps" at colleges and high schools and providing college scholarships.

Key Finding: *States continue to have low overall awareness of risks to their information systems and low confidence in their ability to protect them against cyber threats. State Chief Information Security Officers (CISOs) view a lack of funding and skilled staff as top barriers to improving cybersecurity capabilities.*

A 2012 survey of state CISOs from 48 states and 2 territories found that only 24 percent of these CISOs were confident in their state's ability to protect against external cyber threats.[5] This finding reinforced results from the 2011 Nationwide Cybersecurity Review that indicated that only 36 percent of the 162 state and local government respondents had full awareness of the risks to their information systems. Furthermore, in the 2012 survey, 86 percent of the CISOs indicated that a lack of sufficient funding was the key barrier to addressing their cybersecurity concerns.[6] Similar to many Federal agencies, CISOs also noted that they struggle to attract top cybersecurity talent and develop staff members' skills. In the 2012 SPR results, 78 percent of states and territories confirmed Cybersecurity as a high-priority capability, but only 15 percent rated Cybersecurity training highly, the lowest across all capabilities.

To address these concerns, Federal and state entities are adding new cybersecurity training opportunities for state and local officials. For example, in May 2012, the Texas Engineering Extension Service—a FEMA-sponsored training partner—added face-to-face cybersecurity courses to complement its free online courses. In addition to training investments, DHS's NCCIC continues to encourage state collaboration through the Multi-State Information Sharing and Analysis Center (MS-ISAC), which provides state and local governments with real-time monitoring of their networks, dissemination of early cyber threat warnings, and support to identify and mitigate vulnerabilities to their systems. The MS-ISAC has members in all 50 states and includes technical staff members that direct the Cyber Security Operations Center. An additional tool is the Electricity Subsector Cybersecurity Capability Maturity Model, released by DOE in May 2012. The model allows electric utilities and grid operators to assess their cybersecurity capabilities and prioritize investments to improve cybersecurity. Developed in collaboration with DHS and other industry and Federal partners, the tool combines elements from existing cybersecurity efforts into a common resource for consistent use across the industry.

Preparedness Case Study: Electricity Grid Exercise Tests Preparedness for Cyber Attacks

The North American Electric Reliability Corporation (NERC)—whose mission is to ensure the reliability of the bulk power system—conducted the first-ever, large-scale electricity grid security exercise in November 2011, with 75 industry and government participants from the United States and Canada. The purpose of "GridEx 2011" was to validate the readiness of the electricity industry to respond to a cyber incident, and to validate stakeholder command, control, communication, and crisis response plans. The exercise found that participants effectively applied existing internal security protocols and cyber incident response plans, but also revealed a need for policy updates due to infrastructure upgrades, staff turnover, or new requirements. The exercise also highlighted challenges in sharing information from bulk power system organizations with NERC and government agencies, largely due to compliance concerns.[7]

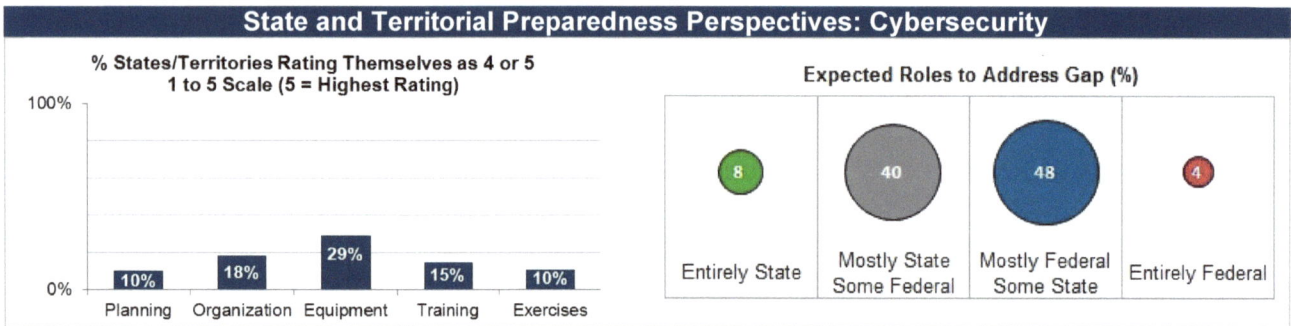

State and Territorial Preparedness Perspectives: Cybersecurity

% States/Territories Rating Themselves as 4 or 5
1 to 5 Scale (5 = Highest Rating)

- Planning: 10%
- Organization: 18%
- Equipment: 29%
- Training: 15%
- Exercises: 10%

Expected Roles to Address Gap (%)

- Entirely State: 8
- Mostly State Some Federal: 40
- Mostly Federal Some State: 48
- Entirely Federal: 4

Physical Protective Measures

The 2012 NPR highlighted previous critical infrastructure assessments that demonstrated owner and operator investments in physical protective measures. Assessments this year showed similar investment trends. Current NPR key findings focus on the role that Protective Security Advisors play in assessing vulnerabilities and facilitating implementation of physical protective and resilience measures at critical infrastructure facilities.

Key Finding: *State, local, tribal, and territorial government partners indicate that Protective Security Advisors (PSAs) are valued resources.*

PSAs from the DHS Office of Infrastructure Protection assist owners and operators of critical infrastructure by coordinating requests for DHS-provided services, such as training, grants, and vulnerability assessments. They also assist state homeland security officials with critical infrastructure protection activities, such as local exercises and planning initiatives. As of February 2013, 95 PSAs and regional directors were located across the 50 states and Puerto Rico, primarily in densely populated areas with many critical infrastructure assets (see Figure 11).

In October 2012, the State, Local, Tribal, and Territorial Government Coordinating Council (SLTTGCC)—comprising homeland security directors from each of these levels of government—published the fifth of nine regionally focused reports on protection programs for critical infrastructure. The reports emphasize the role that PSAs play in helping states and local governments implement their programs. States rely on PSAs to develop relationships with critical infrastructure owners and operators, complete site vulnerability assessments, and offer technical assistance. The SLTTGCC interviewed state officials, who indicated that PSAs are integral members of their homeland security teams. Although Federal support is important to this capability, 82 percent of states and territories indicated that they were mostly or wholly responsible for addressing remaining capability gaps.

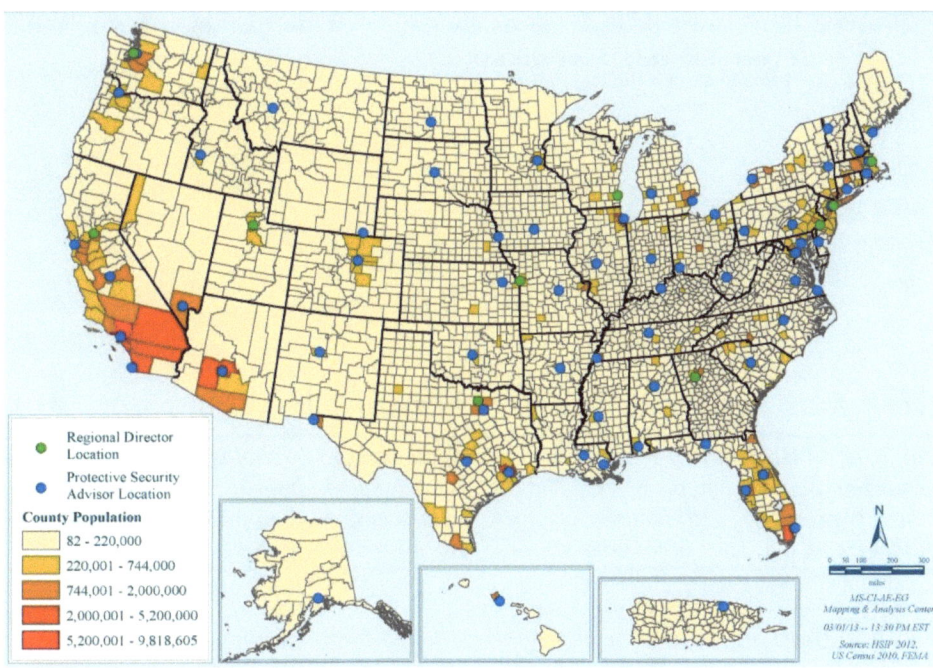

Figure 11: PSAs across the 50 states and Puerto Rico assist states in assessing their infrastructure and implementing their critical infrastructure protection programs.

Key Finding: *DHS continues to expand its infrastructure protection activities to promote more comprehensive, all-hazards approaches to infrastructure resilience.*

Since its creation in 2003, most of DHS's infrastructure efforts have focused on protecting critical infrastructure from potential terrorist threats. Although terrorism remains an important consideration, recent national events have highlighted the significant effects that extreme weather can have on infrastructure. In recognition of this shift, DHS has expanded some infrastructure assessment activities—including the interagency Regional Resiliency Assessment Program (RRAP)—to include all-hazard resilience objectives. Established in 2009, RRAP assessments analyze the resilience of critical infrastructure systems within a particular geographic region. By the end of 2012, the DHS Office of Infrastructure Protection had partnered with stakeholders to complete 27 RRAP assessments, each identifying critical infrastructure dependencies; interdependencies; cascading effects; and state, local, tribal, and territorial capability gaps. DHS is exploring ways to adapt the RRAP process to include emerging issues, such as climate change adaptation and aging infrastructure, while also ensuring that other critical infrastructure activities focus more on resilience. In addition, in February 2013, the President issued *PPD 21: Critical Infrastructure Security and Resilience*, which focuses on clarifying functional relationships, enabling the effective exchange of information among relevant stakeholders, and integrating analysis into planning and operational decision-making related to critical infrastructure.

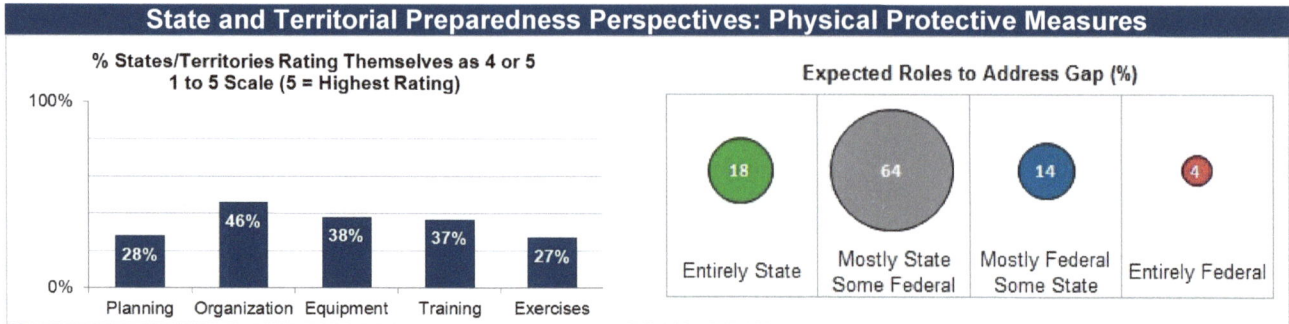

Risk Management for Protection Programs and Activities

The 2012 NPR noted that some public and private-sector stakeholders increasingly use risk to inform their protection policies and programs. The current NPR key findings explore the maturity of state and local programs aimed at protecting critical infrastructure, and examine ways in which the Federal Government supports risk management activities across the Nation.

Key Finding: *States use varying approaches to implement risk management activities outlined under the NIPP, although their ability to measure the effectiveness of critical infrastructure protection program activities remains a challenge.*

As part of its two-year reporting effort, the SLTTGCC conducted interviews with critical infrastructure protection officials in 31 states, and found different approaches in how states were implementing the NIPP's six-step risk management process. For example, some states direct critical infrastructure protection programs at the state level and struggle to extend them to local governments. Other states approach these activities locally. States reporting difficulties in extending programs to local partners cited reduced funding and the lack of scalable DHS programs as barriers.

The SLTTGCC also found that none of the critical infrastructure protection programs it studied could measure the effectiveness of their activities. The group cited the uncertainty of future grant funding and the inherent complexities in assessing the effectiveness of risk mitigation efforts as potential reasons. However, several states are actively attempting to address these challenges. The State of Georgia has collaborated with the Georgia Tech Research Institute to develop methods for measuring the effectiveness of site assessment;, the California Emergency Management Agency is engaged in similar efforts.

Preparedness Case Study: Helping Commercial Facilities Assess Risk

DHS created the Risk Self-Assessment Tool (RSAT) to help owners and operators of commercial facilities assess and manage the risks they face from different threats and hazards. With four new modules in 2011, the free, web-based tool is available to stadiums and arenas, performing arts centers, hotel and lodging facilities, convention centers, racetracks, and amusement and theme parks. Facilities enter basic information (e.g., facility size and capacity, potential threats and hazards, security procedures) into the online tool, which also includes DHS threat and consequence estimates. Customized RSAT reports identify security strengths and vulnerabilities for the facility, outline options for enhanced security measures, and compare results to other buildings of similar size and use. Owners and operators can use RSAT information to identify and prioritize security measures, gaps in procedures, or staff training needs.

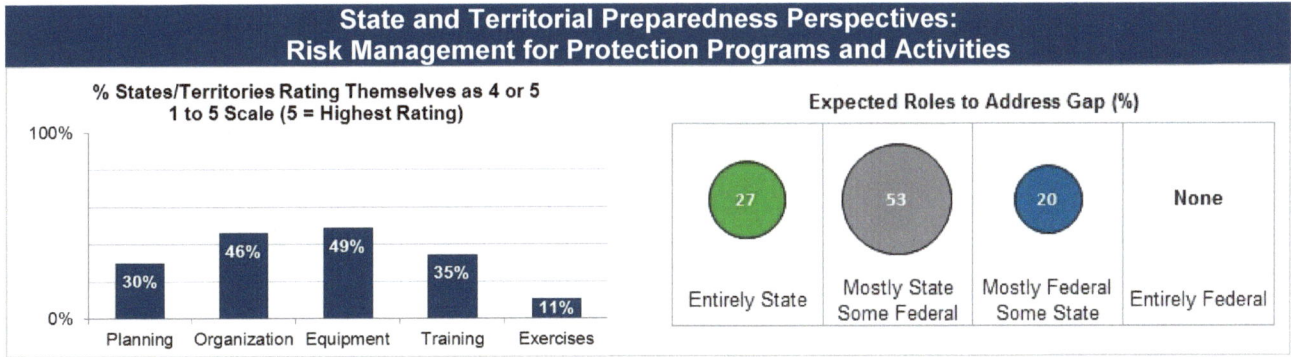

Supply Chain Integrity and Security

The 2012 NPR discussed the success of key government programs in securing critical elements of the global supply chain. Since that time, Federal entities have advanced global supply chain security through initial implementation of 12 action items associated with the 2012 National Strategy for Global Supply Chain Security. *Current NPR findings examine early results from strategy implementation and explore issues related to securing the information technology supply chain.*

Key Finding: *A U.S. Government study characterizing global supply chain risk found an overall resilient system that faces a wide range of threats and hazards.*

As part of the implementation guidance supporting the White House *National Strategy for Global Supply Chain Security*, DHS led an interagency effort in 2012 to characterize risk associated with major disruptions to transportation system elements of the global supply chain. This effort included gathering data on the likelihood and consequences of various scenarios that could potentially cause major supply chain disruptions. The study team considered existing literature and gathered insights from interagency subject matter experts and private-sector and foreign partners to determine that a major global supply chain disruption was not likely. The study group concluded that the greatest potential for a major disruption lies at critical transportation points through which trade flows, such as ports, hubs, and concentrations of critical infrastructure. DHS and its partners continue to refine the risk characterization by filling data gaps and modeling how shocks to the system can escalate from localized events into broader disruptions.

Key Finding: *National security-related agencies have not fully developed supply chain protection measures and risk mitigation strategies to protect against threats to their information systems.*

Federal information systems rely on a global supply chain for production and delivery of their components, including electronic hardware, software, and technical support services. Consequently, these systems remain vulnerable to supply chain threats, such as the installation of counterfeit hardware and software. A March 2012 GAO review of four national security agencies showed wide disparity in addressing risks to the information technology supply chain. Specifically, DOE and DHS had not defined supply chain protection measures for their systems, while DOD and DOJ had identified relevant protection measures, such as maximizing visibility into suppliers and implementing a citizenship and residency requirement. Of these four departments, only DOD had defined procedures for implementation of the protection measures.

To help address these challenges, in 2012, NIST released draft guidance on risk management practices for supply chains for Federal information systems. NIST used international standards and existing government and industry guidance to introduce 10 key practices for managing risk to the supply chain, including identifying unique elements of the supply chain and limiting access and exposure to them. Moreover, agencies have worked to establish enterprise supply chain protection programs, and have engaged with industry partners (e.g., the electricity subsector) to address related supply chain issues across critical infrastructure sectors, using newly developed risk management tools.

State and Territorial Preparedness Perspectives: Supply Chain Integrity and Security[iii]

% States/Territories Rating Themselves as 4 or 5
1 to 5 Scale (5 = Highest Rating)

- Planning 36%
- Organization 52%
- Equipment 42%
- Training 38%
- Exercises 29%

Expected Roles to Address Gap (%)

- Entirely State 11
- Mostly State Some Federal 45
- Mostly Federal Some State 36
- Entirely Federal 9

[iii] In some instances, the percentages displayed in the bubble charts on expected roles to address capability gaps may total slightly more or less than 100 percent due to rounding.

Mitigation Core Capabilities

Community Resilience

The 2012 NPR focused on the involvement of whole community partners in preparedness and mitigation planning, as well as on support for outreach efforts. To extend the analysis, current NPR findings focus attention on progress in individual preparedness and growth in tailored community outreach efforts through Citizen Corps Councils.

Key Finding: *Participation in the National Preparedness Coalition doubled in 2012, but variations persist in public perceptions of risk and awareness of the benefits of preparedness actions.*

Established in 2003, the National Preparedness Coalition is a FEMA-sponsored initiative that encourages individuals and groups to pledge to prepare for disasters and that provides resources and collaboration opportunities. In 2012, coalition membership more than doubled, totaling over 23,000 members from the public and private sectors (see Figure 12). Coalition members led more than 1,500 events and activities in their communities and engaged more than 1.58 million individuals during National Preparedness Month. The website *Ready.gov* also continues to provide easy-to-access preparedness information and resources. Over 5.5 million individuals accessed the site in 2012.

Recent studies point to the public's growing risk awareness and familiarity with local plans, but improvements in individual preparedness and community resilience are still needed. In FEMA's FY 2012 national survey, nearly half of respondents reported familiarity with local hazards and about half expected to experience a natural hazard, continuing a previous upward trend. However, the survey also showed no substantial change in the percentage of respondents reporting that they had

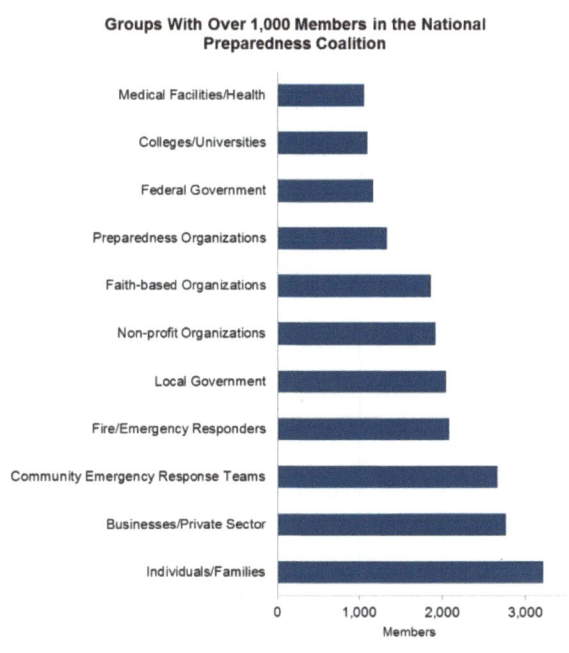

Groups With Over 1,000 Members in the National Preparedness Coalition

Figure 12: In 2012, National Preparedness Coalition membership grew to more than 23,000 members from across the whole community.

made a household emergency plan (43 percent) or built a preparedness kit (52 percent). Recent FEMA surveys show the value of linking public outreach on preparedness to actions taken; people who reported receiving outreach materials were also more likely to attend training, make a kit with disaster supplies, or participate in a preparedness drill.

Public engagement in preparedness activities remains limited, in part because of individual knowledge and perceptions about threats and hazards. For example, a Wharton School survey of over 500 Mid-Atlantic households just prior to Sandy's landfall showed that residents' misperceptions about the storm's risks influenced their preparedness actions.[8] Although most residents took basic actions to prepare, such as assembling supplies (75 percent), only 19 percent planned to heed evacuation advisories. In addition, only 54 percent of those living within one block of a body of water reported having flood insurance.

Key Finding: *Citizen Corps Councils are serving more of the U.S. population by engaging the whole community in planning, tailoring preparedness education and training, and connecting with volunteers to prepare for and respond to emergencies.*

Citizen Corps Councils bring whole community representatives together and support programs to make communities safer and better prepared for emergencies. Over 90 new Councils registered in FY 2012, bringing the total registered Councils to nearly 1,200 locations nationwide. Councils now serve 63 percent of the U.S. population, an increase from 58 percent in September 2011. Recent accomplishments highlighted in 2012 registration data include the following:

- Over 830 Councils (71 percent) reviewed their jurisdictions' key emergency plans and 60 percent of Councils include participation from the public sector, private sector, and community volunteers.

- Councils increased support for community-level education and training in 2012: 73 percent delivered materials or training in neighborhoods, 72 percent in schools, 64 percent in workplaces, and 54 percent in places of worship.

- Councils provided tailored materials and training to individuals with access and functional needs (60 percent), the elderly (57 percent), pet owners (54 percent), and youth (54 percent).

- Volunteer support for response increased in 2012. Over 930 Councils (nearly 80 percent) reported using volunteers to respond to disasters. An additional 400 Community Emergency Response Team (CERT) Programs registered in 2012. This growth raised the number of CERT Program locations to nearly 2,170 nationwide, reflecting approximately 100,000 more CERTs trained in 2012, and a total of 526,670 individuals trained.

Preparedness Case Study: FEMA Corps Supports Disaster Responses

Created in 2012, FEMA Corps is a cadre of service members, aged 18 to 24, who elect to serve up to two years supporting disaster preparedness, response, and recovery efforts. Members receive training and experience toward careers in emergency management and related fields, while fortifying FEMA's workforce with reliable and cost-effective personnel. FEMA Corps will ultimately include 1,600 members. After Sandy, 42 FEMA Corps teams (438 members total) supported community relations activities in New York and New Jersey, providing assistance at Disaster Recovery Centers and traveling door-to-door in affected areas to connect residents to available aid.

State and Territorial Preparedness Perspectives: Community Resilience

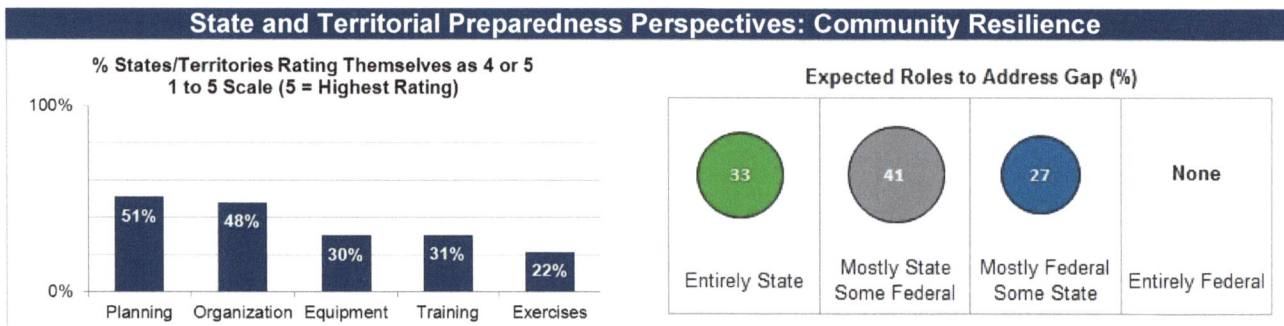

Long-term Vulnerability Reduction

The 2012 NPR highlighted progress in state and local adoption of building codes and flood plain management practices to reduce long-term vulnerability to diverse threats and hazards. Nationwide progress has continued, with FEMA-approved mitigation plans covering over 71 percent of the U.S. population as of 2012. Current NPR findings outline continued activities in these areas.

Key Finding: *Federal mitigation grants and programs reduce the long-term vulnerability of communities to flooding, but tribal participation lags.*

Floods are the most common natural disaster in the United States and cause an average of $7.8 billion in damages and an average of 94 deaths each year. FEMA provides hazard mitigation assistance grants to state and local communities to reduce vulnerability through activities such as property demolition, relocation, elevation, and floodproofing. FEMA estimates that $252 million in grant funds for hazard mitigation assistance, provided to over 1,300 properties nationally in FY 2011, resulted in $502 million in avoided flood losses.

Federal programs also help to reduce vulnerability to and the effects of floods at the community level. For example, the U.S. Army Corps of Engineers (USACE) contributes to national flood risk management by providing technical and planning support to states; inspecting and rehabilitating levees and other flood risk management infrastructure; and alleviating the consequences of flooding events. USACE also participates in Silver Jackets teams, which are interagency partnerships involving state and Federal personnel to reduce flood risk. Silver Jacket teams at the state level coordinate multi-agency mitigation assistance and enhance communication among stakeholders seeking to manage flood risk. As of December 2012, 35 Silver Jackets teams were active across the country, up from 23 the previous year.

In addition, in FY 2011, the National Flood Insurance Program (NFIP) added 9,000 new flood insurance policy holders; continued transitioning to newer, more accurate flood maps; and increased participation in its Community Rating System (CRS) program, which reduces insurance premiums in communities that establish floodplain management programs. As of May 2012, NFIP participation included over 21,700 communities nationwide, and CRS participation had grown approximately four percent from the previous year to more than 1,200 communities. However, only 7 percent of federally recognized tribes participate in the NFIP, with rural locations, lack of administrative resources, and varying land use ordinances contributing to low participation. FEMA has conducted some outreach with tribal partners, largely through training and technical assistance, as well as marketing through the NFIP FloodSmart campaign.

Preparedness Case Study: Mitigation Investments Protect New Orleans

After the catastrophic failure of the New Orleans levee system following Hurricane Katrina, USACE initiated a $14.6 billion reconstruction and mitigation project in southeast Louisiana, called the Hurricane and Storm Damage Risk Reduction System. The multi-year project strengthened the levees, floodwalls, pump stations, and surge barriers that form the 133-mile Greater New Orleans perimeter system, preparing it to defend against a 100-year storm. The system performed successfully and protected the region during Mississippi River flooding in spring 2011 and Hurricane Isaac in summer 2012. In New Orleans, the system is estimated to have prevented $68 billion in damages during the spring flooding and protected 840,000 residents during Hurricane Isaac.

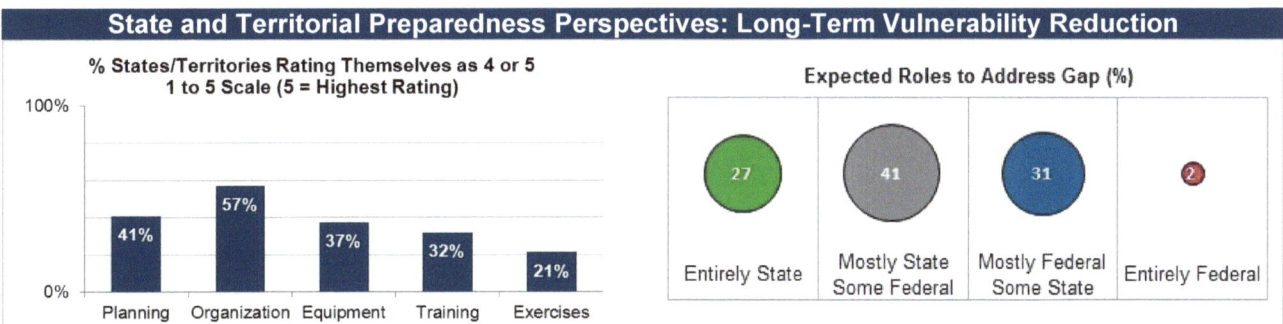

State and Territorial Preparedness Perspectives: Long-Term Vulnerability Reduction

% States/Territories Rating Themselves as 4 or 5
1 to 5 Scale (5 = Highest Rating)

Planning 41% · Organization 57% · Equipment 37% · Training 32% · Exercises 21%

Expected Roles to Address Gap (%)

Entirely State 27 · Mostly State Some Federal 41 · Mostly Federal Some State 31 · Entirely Federal 2

Risk and Disaster Resilience Assessment

The 2012 NPR highlighted well-established national processes aimed at identifying hazards and assessing risk. These efforts include training programs for natural and other threats and hazards, as well as software tools and user groups. The current NPR explores the growing specialization and integration of risk assessment tools.

Key Finding: *Specialized national-level geographic information systems assist risk assessment planning for tsunamis, earthquakes, and floods.*

Risk assessment tools for various natural hazards—including tsunamis, earthquakes, and floods—help to planners factor risk into their processes. For example, the National Oceanic and Atmospheric Administration (NOAA) enhanced tsunami forecasting models and associated inundation and evacuation maps. A 2011 National Research Council report on tsunami warning and preparedness highlighted progress, but recommended that NOAA and the National Tsunami Hazard Mitigation Program develop national guidelines and measures for tsunami preparedness.[9] The U.S. Geological Survey (USGS) assesses earthquake risk to people, property, and infrastructure using ShakeMaps—probabilistic and scenario-based ground-motion hazard maps. Jurisdictions can use these maps to inform response and recovery activities, as well as ongoing planning efforts. Through these tools, the USGS estimates that 75 million people in 39 states are subject to "significant risk" from earthquakes.

In addition, FEMA's Risk Mapping, Assessment, and Planning (Risk MAP) program supports planners with modeling software and floodplain data. The public and private sectors use these National Flood Insurance Rate Maps an estimated 30 million times annually, overlaying historical flood probabilities with current structures and populations. In FY 2011, Risk MAP added 385 projects, affecting 5,100 communities and covering 40 percent of the U.S. population living in watersheds. Moreover, 51 percent of Risk MAP data now meets more accurate standards and incorporates digital topography.

Recognition is growing that less predictable and/or more severe natural hazards could challenge the use of historical data to assess future risk. Scientific observations have captured a host of changes in historical data patterns, including sea ice melt, temperature rise, and frequency and intensity of heavy precipitation. Recognizing the need to adapt to emerging trends, FEMA's Strategic Foresight Initiative has encouraged the whole community to consider how changes in extreme weather patterns—in combination with other drivers such as growing urban and coastal populations and aging infrastructure—may lead to a need for more extensive mitigation and emergency response actions.

Preparedness Case Study: USCG Prepares for Maritime Changes in the Arctic

The Arctic presents unique operating challenges, including limited infrastructure in a large and remote geographical area with increasing economic activity; logistical challenges due to extreme weather; and a changing climate. To reduce long-term vulnerability to Arctic residents, businesses, and visitors, the USCG conducted Operation Arctic Shield in 2012. Participants assessed operations and mission support capabilities in Arctic conditions; conducted outreach to Arctic communities; and deployed major cutter forces, air assets, communications equipment, and mission support for USCG missions. Arctic Shield also included an oil spill-contingency exercise to test USCG and U.S. Navy skimming equipment. Lessons learned from Arctic Shield are shaping USCG planning and strategy to ensure long-term safety, security, and stewardship of the emerging Arctic maritime frontier.

State and Territorial Preparedness Perspectives: Risk and Disaster Resilience Assessment

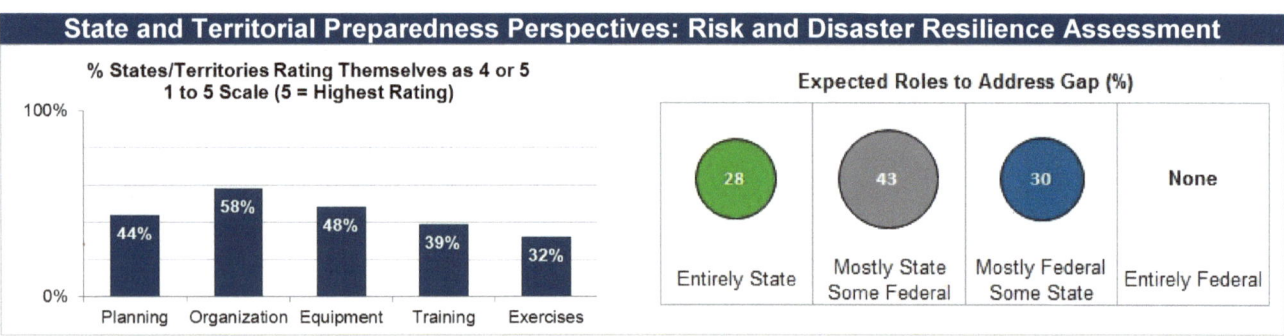

Threats and Hazard Identification

The 2012 NPR confirmed that whole community partners increasingly incorporate threat and hazard information into risk-based planning, taking into consideration event frequency and magnitude in order to more clearly understand community needs. The current NPR explores implementation of new planning guidance.

Key Finding: *New Federal guidance on threat and hazard identification helps states and urban areas document risks, evaluate event consequences, and set capability targets.*

Through the FY 2012 Homeland Security Grant Program, FEMA required all 56 states and territories and 31 urban areas to submit THIRAs to establish a picture of state and local risk across the Nation. In addition, in April 2012, FEMA published *Comprehensive Preparedness Guide 201: THIRA Guide*, which outlined a common process for developing high-consequence threat and hazard scenarios with national impacts. In fulfillment of this new requirement, 48 states and 27 urban areas submitted THIRA information to FEMA in December 2012. A number of these first-ever THIRA submissions highlighted threats and hazards that triggered cascading effects, with an initial threat or hazard causing follow-on events. Example scenarios included earthquakes triggering tsunamis, or cyber attacks leading to power outages and other infrastructure failures.

Through the THIRA process, states and local jurisdictions estimate event consequences and set capability targets based on an incident that will most challenge the capability. Ultimately, capability targets help states identify the resources needed for each of the 31 core capabilities to prevent, protect against, mitigate, respond to, and recover from high-consequence events. State and local decision-makers assess current capabilities relative to these targets and use the results to address identified gaps. Furthermore, THIRA development represents a major step forward in the National Preparedness System, allowing state and local jurisdictions to make risk-informed decisions based on their unique threats and hazards. Overall, 86 percent of states and territories indicated that they were mostly or wholly responsible for addressing remaining gaps in this capability.

Preparedness Case Study: Environmental Protection Agency (EPA) Amendments Improve Hazard Identification Data

The Emergency Planning and Community Right-to-Know Act (EPCRA) requires communities to develop comprehensive emergency plans that address risks posed by chemical hazards present in their communities. The act also requires facilities to report on the presence of extremely hazardous substances and hazardous chemicals, as well as releases of toxic chemicals. In July 2012, the EPA finalized amendments to EPCRA regulations that modify existing data reporting requirements for facilities. Specifically, in response to stakeholder requests, EPA added new data elements to hazardous chemical inventory forms to better inform community emergency response plans, and revised other data elements to make reporting easier for facilities.

State and Territorial Preparedness Perspectives: Threats and Hazard Identification

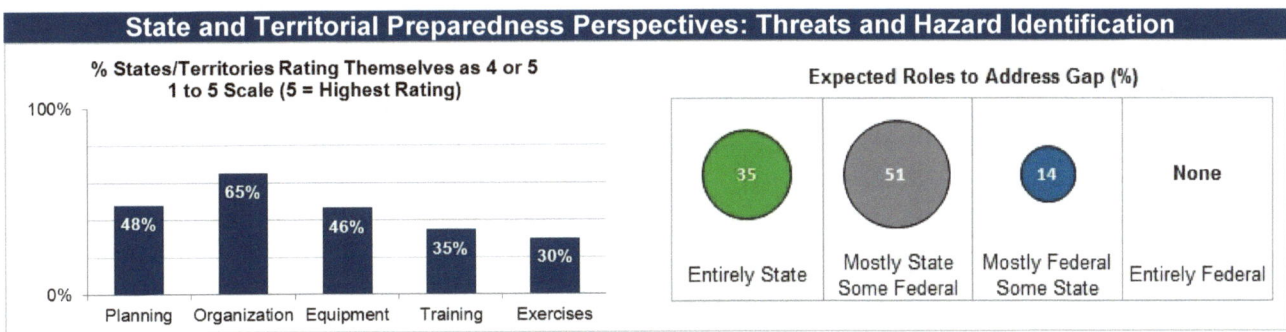

% States/Territories Rating Themselves as 4 or 5
1 to 5 Scale (5 = Highest Rating)

Planning: 48%
Organization: 65%
Equipment: 46%
Training: 35%
Exercises: 30%

Expected Roles to Address Gap (%)

Entirely State: 35
Mostly State Some Federal: 51
Mostly Federal Some State: 14
Entirely Federal: None

Response Core Capabilities

Critical Transportation

The Nation maintains mature capabilities to manage logistics and repair emergency transportation infrastructure, as outlined in the 2012 NPR. The current NPR explores state and local efforts to enforce mandatory evacuations.

Key finding: *Sandy illustrated ongoing challenges associated with issuing and enforcing evacuation orders.*

Mandatory evacuation orders issued to protect residents in advance of major disasters present challenges in messaging and enforcement for state and local officials. Even though public officials such as the Mayor of New York City and Governor of New Jersey ordered the evacuation of almost half a million residents before the storm, hundreds of thousands disregarded the orders. In New York City, 35 of the 43 storm-related deaths resulted from drowning, largely in areas under mandatory evacuation orders. Officials in New York and New Jersey chose not to enforce evacuation orders through arrests but appealed to the public to leave.[10, 11]

Numerous studies have explored the challenges associated with issuing and enforcing evacuation orders. For example, researchers surveyed residents of North Carolina and Massachusetts following Hurricane Earl (2010) and of New Jersey following Hurricane Irene (2011) in order to understand residents' decision-making processes in the face of disasters.[12,13] These studies found that residents who made plans to evacuate did so primarily as a result of notices from public officials. Additionally, the South Carolina Emergency Management Division—in coordination with the USACE and the University of South Carolina—conducted a behavioral study of coastal residents that found that the use of mandatory evacuation orders increases the likelihood of residents evacuating for Category 1 or Category 2 storms by 25 percent.[14] The authority to order mandatory evacuations lies with different levels of government across the Nation, as outlined in Figure 13. Figure 14 illustrates that states levy a variety of penalties to enforce evacuation orders.[15] However, few states enforce these penalties in practice.

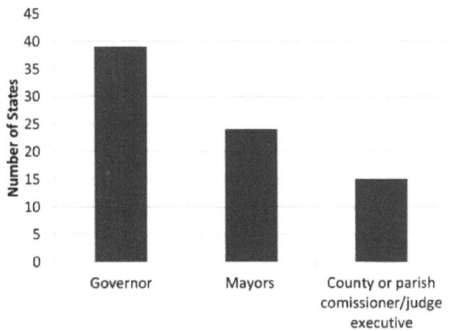

Figure 13: Authority to order mandatory evacuation varies across the country.

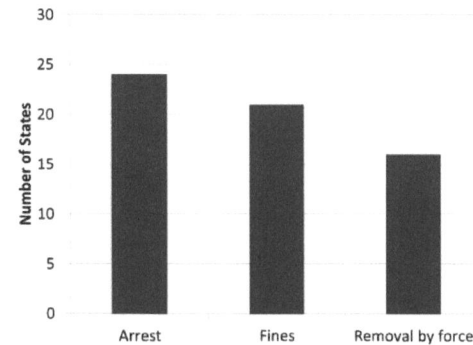

Figure 14: States have a variety of penalties in place to enforce mandatory evacuation orders.

Preparedness Case Study: Addressing Water Removal and Power Needs Post-Sandy

One major challenge experienced after Sandy involved the unprecedented flooding of major transportation routes into and out of Manhattan. USACE had a cadre of responders and pre-established Navy contracting processes in place with FEMA, enabling a prompt and agile response. Before landfall, USACE began coordinating with the State of New York and New York City regarding plans for potential water-removal requirements. After landfall, USACE deployed on receipt of a verbal assignment from FEMA to begin water-removal and emergency power-generation missions quickly. USACE personnel, along with partners from the Navy Supervisor of Salvage and USCG, were instrumental to restoring major transportation arteries, including the Brooklyn-Battery Tunnel and the Jersey City Port Authority Trans-Hudson Train Tunnel. Overall, more than 4,000 USACE personnel supported response efforts in New York and New Jersey. USACE completed pumping missions by November 10, 2012, using 162 pumps to remove over 260 million gallons of water from tunnels, water treatment plants, and other inundated areas.

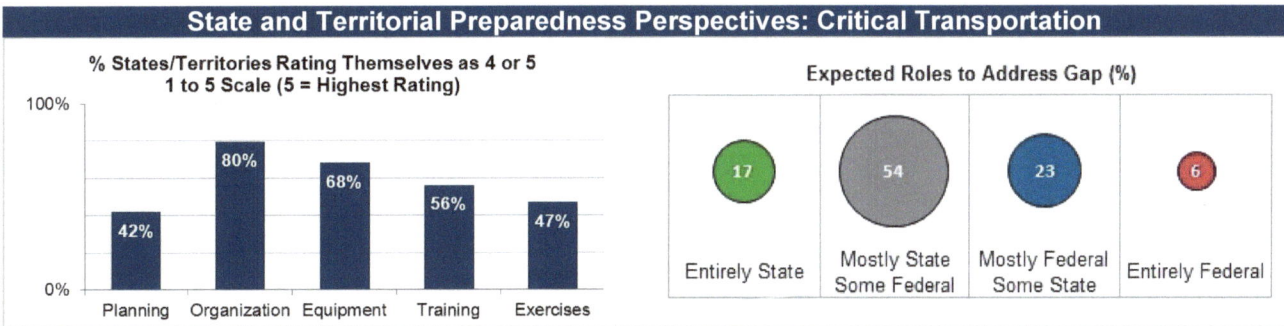

State and Territorial Preparedness Perspectives: Critical Transportation

% States/Territories Rating Themselves as 4 or 5
1 to 5 Scale (5 = Highest Rating)

Planning 42% | Organization 80% | Equipment 68% | Training 56% | Exercises 47%

Expected Roles to Address Gap (%)

Entirely State 17 | Mostly State Some Federal 54 | Mostly Federal Some State 23 | Entirely Federal 6

Environmental Response/Health and Safety

The Nation maintains mature assets for environmental response/health and safety for conventional hazardous materials incidents and continues to build specialized response capabilities for CBRNE incidents, as outlined in the 2012 NPR. Current NPR findings provide an update on the status of DOD resources for CBRNE response operations, as well as on efforts to integrate these specialized capabilities with other response resources.

Key Finding: *The DOD Chemical, Biological, Radiological, Nuclear (CBRN) Response Enterprise reached full operational capability in October 2012, providing over 18,000 personnel capable of supporting and conducting operations in CBRN environments. Effective integration of the CBRN Response Enterprise with Federal, state, and local resources remains a priority.*

The DOD CBRN Response Enterprise includes the Defense CBRN Response Force (DCRF); two Command and Control CBRN Response Elements (C2CRE); 57 National Guard Weapons of Mass Destruction (WMD) Civil Support Teams; 17 National Guard CBRNE Enhanced Response Force Packages (CERFPs); and 10 newly established Homeland Response Forces (HRFs). Together, these units provide approximately 18,000 personnel capable of supporting and conducting operations in CBRN environments.

The HRFs, established in FY 2011 with approximately 566 personnel in total, provide command and control and support personnel, with additional search and extraction, medical, and decontamination capabilities that mirror a CERFP. The HRFs can respond within 6 to 12 hours of an event and deliver rapid, scalable capability that bridges the gap between the initial response of WMD Civil Support Teams and CERFPs under state control, and the later response of the DCRF and C2CRE under Federal control. In FY 2012, the National Guard finished establishing one HRF in each of the 10 FEMA Regions. DOD's strategic positioning of WMD Civil Support Teams, CERFPs, and HRFs ensures that 80 percent of the U.S. population is within 250 miles of one of these assets.

The range of entities comprising the CBRN Response Enterprise underscore the need to effectively integrate these elements with Federal, state, and local response assets. For example, a December 2011 GAO report noted that most CERFPs have had limited opportunities to train with interagency partners. Specifically, in states with CERFPs, an average of 43 percent of state emergency management agencies conducted annual training with CERFPs each year between 2008 and 2010. Recently, in July and August 2012, U.S. Northern Command conducted the Vibrant Response 13 exercise to bring together Federal, state, and local agencies and to confirm the readiness of the DCRF and C2CRE. More than 9,000 service members and civilians participated in 200 separate training events (addressing a simulated 10-kiloton nuclear detonation in a major Midwestern city), held over 19 days at 50 different locations.

Key Finding: *The Nation lacks capabilities for cleanup activities following large-scale biological attacks.*

In an October 2011 report assessing the Nation's bioresponse capabilities, the Bipartisan WMD Terrorism Research Center found that the Nation made considerable progress developing capabilities for small-scale, indoor cleanup of biological agents (e.g., anthrax), but that it still lacks the capability to remediate a large-scale, wide-area release.[16] For example, fumigation technologies developed to decontaminate buildings do not apply to outdoor environments.[17] Additional challenges include unclear Federal roles and responsibilities; unresolved scientific and technical issues (e.g., secondary aerosolization); a lack of resources for sampling, testing, and analysis; the absence of decontamination standards; insufficient quantities of private decontamination contractors; and an absence of policies and guidance for privately owned facilities.[18,19]

In May 2011, DHS published *Interim Consequence Management Guidance for a Wide-Area Biological Attack*, which has supported two regional planning efforts. In 2012, a partnership between DHS and DOD, in coordination with the Denver Urban Area Security Initiative, produced preliminary tools and a planning framework for reducing the time and resources needed to return functionality to a large urban area following a chemical, biological, or radiological incident. In addition, in 2012, Federal partners with expertise in biodefense, infectious diseases, and occupational health and safety developed and published guidance to protect responders following a wide-area anthrax attack.

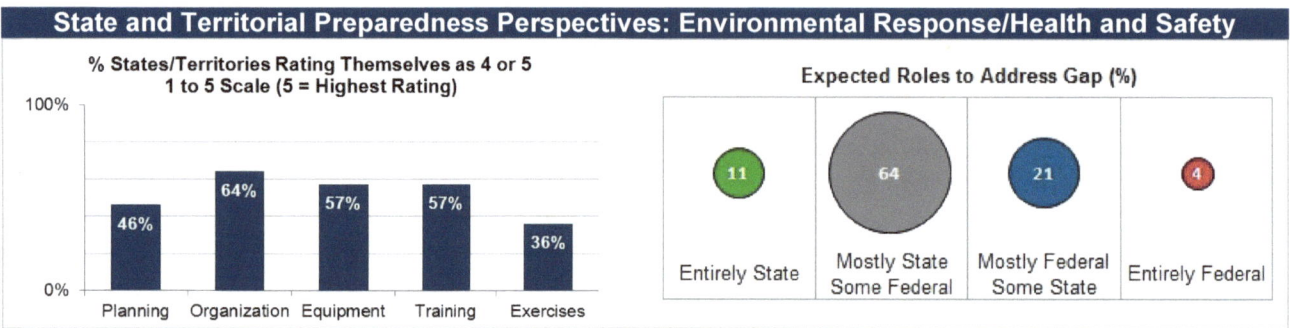

State and Territorial Preparedness Perspectives: Environmental Response/Health and Safety

% States/Territories Rating Themselves as 4 or 5
1 to 5 Scale (5 = Highest Rating)

Planning 46%, Organization 64%, Equipment 57%, Training 57%, Exercises 36%

Expected Roles to Address Gap (%)

Entirely State 11, Mostly State Some Federal 64, Mostly Federal Some State 21, Entirely Federal 4

Fatality Management Services

As outlined in the 2012 NPR, Federal assets such as Disaster Mortuary Operational Response Teams and Fatality Search and Recovery Teams support state and local jurisdiction needs in large-scale disasters. However, state and local coroners and medical examiners address the majority of mass fatality events without Federal involvement. This year's NPR examines efforts to develop and support state and local capabilities for fatality management.

Key Finding: *Some states and localities have taken the initiative to plan, train, and develop resources for mass fatality events. In addition, Federal agencies have taken recent steps to support the development of state and local capability through additional guidance and leadership.*

Mass fatality management has received inconsistent attention nationwide. Between FY 2006 and FY 2011, only 24 out of 56 states and territories invested DHS preparedness grant funding in fatality management activities, totaling less than $32 million. States and territories rated Fatality Management Services as the weakest among all Response mission area capabilities in the 2012 SPR.

Even so, selected areas of the country have made notable progress. Jurisdictions such as New York City, Harris County (Houston, Texas), and Florida have served as planning forerunners. For example, in April 2011, the Florida Emergency Mortuary Operations Response System developed a concept of operations to help respond to and manage fatalities in a CBRN environment.[20] Moreover, organizations nationwide have requested training related to mass fatality. The National Transportation Safety Board (NTSB) alone held 49 outreach presentations in the past two years (see Figure 15). Furthermore, some states—including Alabama, Florida, Iowa, Missouri, Ohio, and Texas—have established their own mass fatality teams. The New York City Office of Chief Medical Examiner has also developed an integrated, web-based system— the Unified Victim Identification System—to manage missing persons and victim identification. Developed with DHS grant funding, this system is available at no-cost to jurisdictions. As of the end of 2012, the system is operational in three states, with licenses issued or pending in 15 others.[21]

Historically, Federal guidance to state and local jurisdictions for mass fatality management was limited, and there was no dedicated role in place for a Federal program coordinator. Over the past three years, however, Federal agencies have made progress in these areas. In 2010, the FBI established the Scientific Working Group on Disaster Victim Identification, which brings together subject matter experts to develop guidelines and best practices for identifying disaster victims. In 2011 and 2012, the CDC and ASPR issued national standards for state and local planning in 17 health and medical core capabilities, including fatality management. In 2012, HHS hired its first, full-time national program

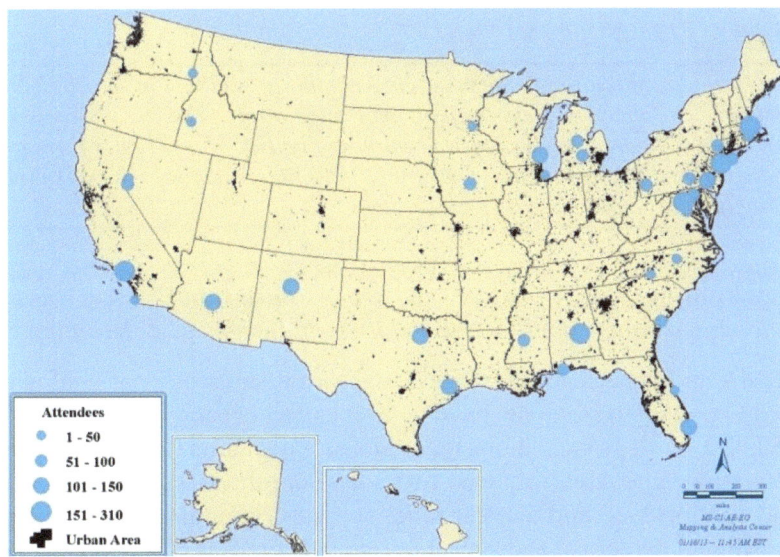

Figure 15: In 2011 and 2012, NTSB conducted outreach presentations in 40 locations nationwide, instructing over 3,600 attendees on family assistance and mass fatality management issues following transportation disasters.

coordinator for fatality management, and finalized its fatality management concept of operations, which outlines the approach for managing mass fatalities in disasters that result in fewer than 5,000 fatalities.

Preparedness Case Study: Conducting Regional Mass Fatality Exercises

The Regional Catastrophic Planning Team for New York, New Jersey, Connecticut, and Pennsylvania has produced the *Regional Mass Fatality Management Response System Plan*, which establishes a regional response system to coordinate resources, provide expertise and operational support, and streamline decision-making among multiple stakeholders.[22] In partnership with county medical examiner offices, the Regional Mass Fatality Management System holds an annual training and exercise event to practice the Plan and prepare regional partners for their respective roles in a mass fatality incident. The scenario for the 2012 exercise (in Dutchess County, New York) involved a collision between a fuel tanker and a commuter train. Participants included local agencies, the NTSB, Air National Guard Fatality Search and Recovery Teams, the 49th Quartermaster Group, the FBI, and various regional partners.[23] The trainings and exercises have improved cohesiveness and collaboration, identified leaders and critical assets, and highlighted issues and best practices. Lessons learned include ensuring interoperable communication systems with partner jurisdictions, purchasing interoperable equipment for response flexibility and scale-up, and standardizing protocols.

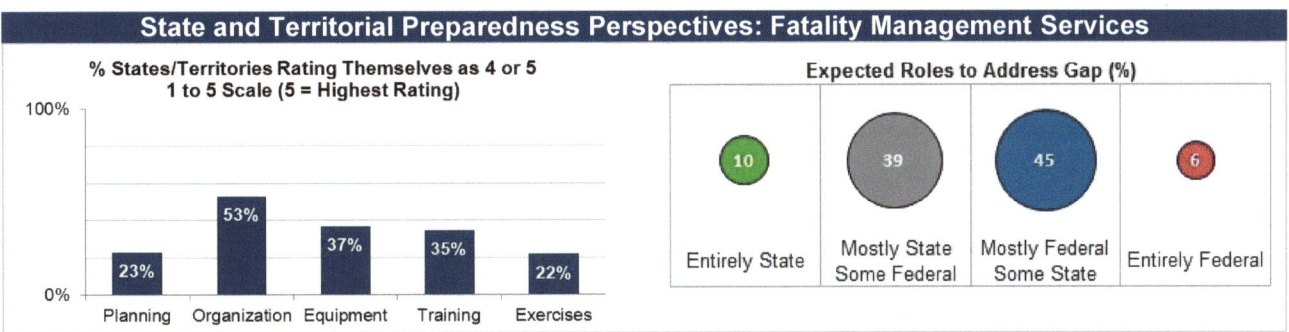

Mass Care Services

The Nation is maintaining the mass care resources outlined in the 2012 NPR and is improving the delivery of mass care services after disasters through implementation of the 2012 National Mass Care Strategy. *The Nation also continues to address challenges in reuniting families post-disaster through the development of national guidance and various tracking systems. Current NPR findings explore how stakeholders from the whole community collaborate to improve mass care services.*

Key Finding: *Public and private partners have significant resources to support mass care services following a catastrophic event, but face challenges in distributing them.*

FEMA and American Red Cross databases document a national network of 63,000 shelters. American Red Cross shelters, alone, have an evacuation capacity of over 3 million, and a post-impact capacity of 850,000. Both organizations maintain supply chains to support shelter residents in the event of shelter activation. The American Red Cross has supplies to support 350,000 shelter residents (e.g., cots, blankets, and comfort kits) and disaster relief supplies (including home cleanup kits, shovels, rakes, work gloves, flashlights, batteries, and sunscreen) to support 500,000 people. The Federal Government also maintains additional shelter supplies. The General Services Administration (GSA) can deliver up to 100,000 standard cots, 100,000 tarps, and 150,000 hygiene kits within three days of an event.

Following Sandy, response efforts required many of these resources when 8.5 million customers lost power along the East Coast. While the peak shelter population totaled 25,000 across the 10 affected states, many more survivors required feeding, hydration, and disaster relief supplies. FEMA and its Emergency Support Function (ESF) #6 (Mass Care) partners provided over 4 million liters of water and 6 million meals in the week after the storm. In addition, the Maritime Administration provided three ships to house and feed more than 1,150 disaster relief personnel, freeing up area lodging and improving access for disaster personnel to survivors in New York City. However, challenges arose in locating and distributing resources to some survivors, such as residents stranded in powerless, high-rise public housing buildings. Maintaining situational awareness of health conditions and needs of persons housed in shelters remains a challenge, requiring additional surveillance tools and reporting systems.

Preparedness Case Study: Public-Private Partnerships Deliver Pet Response Capabilities

Since the passage of the Pets Evacuation and Transportation Standards Act of 2006, FEMA, USDA, HHS, and non-governmental partners—including the National Animal Rescue and Sheltering Coalition and the National Alliance of State Animal and Agricultural Emergency Programs—have collaborated in strategic planning and preparedness activities. These actions came to fruition in response to Sandy. Two days before the storm, the New York State Department of Agriculture and Markets staged temporary animal sheltering resources with the American Society for the Prevention of Cruelty to Animals (ASPCA) and PetSmart Charities. In New York City, the ASPCA set up a free boarding facility with the New York City Office of Emergency Management and the New York City Animal Protection Task Force. The National Veterinary Response Teams of the National Disaster Medical System provided veterinary medical support for the shelter. Partners coordinated receipt and distribution of 421 tons of pet food and supplies donated by pet food manufacturers to pet owners, staging areas, points of distribution, and food banks in the affected areas.

Key finding: *The Federal Government is enhancing mass care services for individuals with disabilities and with access and functional needs, while investing in research to identify how to keep medical equipment and other assistive devices running through prolonged power outages.*

In late 2010, FEMA released guidance on integrating functional needs support services in mass care shelters, following challenges experienced during Hurricane Ike. Since February 2011, FEMA has improved functional needs support services by streamlining internal procedures and issuing specialized kits with equipment for infants, toddlers, and individuals with disabilities. FEMA also awarded contracts to provide personal assistance services in mass care shelters to individuals with disabilities and access and functional needs. First tested after Sandy, these contracts enable general population shelter operators to provide services to disaster survivors, such as grooming, bathing, and medication administration. The June 2012 derecho on the East Coast and Sandy both highlighted how prolonged power outages present mass care challenges for individuals who rely on electricity to run medical equipment or other assistance devices required to maintain independent living situations. In response, FEMA and HHS are partnering to research technologies that will allow individuals needing electrically-powered durable medical equipment (e.g., ventilators, suction pumps) or other assistive devices (e.g., power wheelchairs, augmentative communication devices) to use their equipment through a prolonged power outage.

Whole Community Case Study: Engaging Veteran Volunteers Through Team Rubicon

Founded in 2010 in response to the Haiti earthquake, Team Rubicon's mission is to "bridge the gap" between when a disaster occurs and when traditional aid organizations can respond, by providing rapidly-deployable response teams composed primarily of military veterans. The nonprofit organization was founded on the premise that the skills veterans gain during their military service (e.g., logistics, emergency medicine, risk assessment) are also valuable during disaster response. In its largest operation to date, Team Rubicon deployed more than 300 military veterans to Far Rockaway, New York, in response to Sandy. They supported search and rescue operations, removed debris from homes, delivered emergency supplies, managed over 5,000 volunteers, and provided medical aid.

State and Territorial Preparedness Perspectives: Mass Care Services

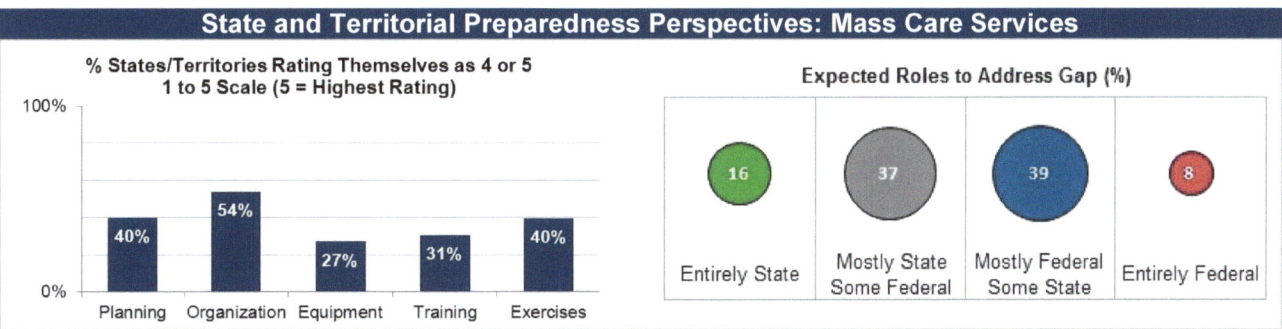

Mass Search and Rescue Operations

The 2012 NPR highlighted the Nation's mature capabilities in structural collapse search and rescue (SAR) efforts, as well as its inland and maritime SAR resources that support disaster response. A mass search and rescue event, such as a catastrophic earthquake, would require a surge in SAR resources beyond traditionally available sources. The current NPR focuses on strategies to augment response capacity and to integrate non-traditional resources into mass SAR efforts.

Key Finding: *While many Federal agencies support SAR efforts, a catastrophic event will require significant military and community-based involvement.*

FEMA, the National Park Service, the Air Force Rescue Coordination Center, and the USCG collectively assign or carry out tens of thousands of search and rescue missions each year in urban, inland, and maritime/coastal environments. These missions rarely require immediate response for large numbers of distressed people. However, a single catastrophic event may require wellness checks of hundreds of thousands of structures across multiple states, exceeding the capacity of these traditional search and rescue assets.

The National Guard provides additional surge capacity to address SAR needs in catastrophic events. To assist civilian authorities in affected states, more than 87,000 National Guard members under state control, 75 inflatable boats, 3,125 high-water vehicles, 726 debris-clearance vehicles, and 140 rotary-winged aircraft are potentially accessible from other states. Moreover, U.S. Northern Command—in collaboration with FEMA, the National Guard Bureau, and other stakeholders—issued a concept of operations in June 2011 that addresses how states' National Guard members and Federal active-duty military units can add SAR capacity during a catastrophe. The concept of operations covers both military personnel trained in SAR practices and personnel without specific SAR training, but who have capabilities that may be useful in a SAR situation.

In addition, community volunteers can supplement mass search and rescue capacity. Across the country, CERT Programs train individuals in basic response skills, such as light search and rescue. CERT Programs are increasingly prepared to deliver rapid SAR capability when professional responders are not immediately available. In a 2012 survey, 1,383 CERT Programs reported that they had responded to at least one emergency. Of these, 718 CERT Programs (52 percent) reported that they had provided residential and neighborhood checks in response to emergencies, and almost 400 CERT Programs (29 percent) reported that local teams had supported basic search and rescue activities during an emergency.

Preparedness Case Study: SAR Efforts in Sandy

Prior to Sandy's landfall, the USCG deployed aircraft and cutters in response to the sinking of the HMS Bounty 90 miles southeast of Cape Hatteras, North Carolina. The USCG saved 14 people from the 16-person crew and searched more than 90 hours and over 12,000 nautical square miles for the ship's missing captain. In addition, in response to Sandy, FEMA deployed nine Urban Search and Rescue (US&R) Task Forces that searched more than 47,000 structures and assisted more than 1,200 survivors. Sandy also required activating recently acquired capabilities (e.g., equipment, training) to conduct search and rescue operations in flooded environments and in those contaminated with hazardous materials. In addition, FEMA established a Federal Search and Rescue Coordination Group, which facilitated communications and information sharing between Federal, state, local, and tribal search and rescue providers, and delivered a coordinated Federal SAR response in the storm's aftermath.

State and Territorial Preparedness Perspectives: Mass Search and Rescue Operations

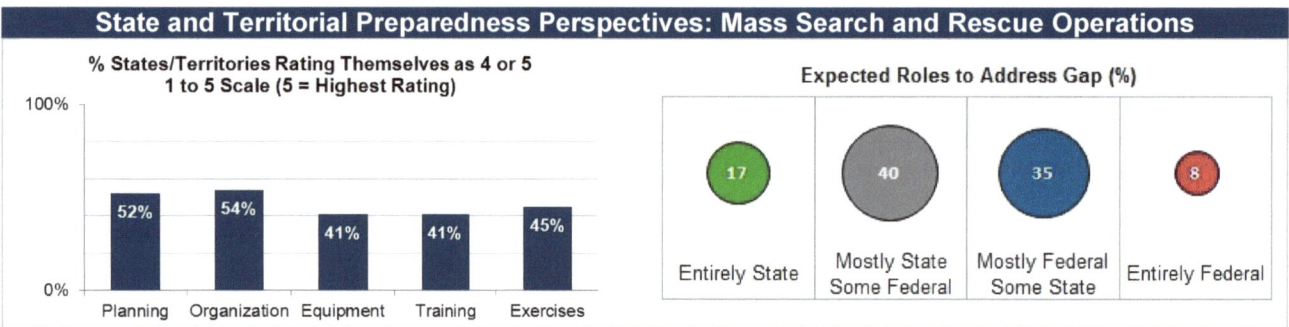

On-scene Security and Protection

The 2012 NPR demonstrated that state and local law enforcement agencies provide the foundation for security and protection operations nationally. The current NPR explores how Federal law enforcement support to states and localities is evolving.

Key Finding: *State, local, tribal, and territorial law enforcement agencies can draw on a wide range of Federal law enforcement assets during disasters. However, processes for supplying Federal law enforcement support are still maturing.*

ESF #13 (Public Safety and Security) coordinates Federal support to incidents that have exhausted state, local, tribal, or territorial law enforcement assets. ESF #13 draws from the wide range of law enforcement officers across the Federal Government. In the aftermath of Sandy, over 250 Federal law enforcement officers—from the Bureau of Alcohol, Tobacco, Firearms and Explosives; Drug Enforcement Administration; Federal Air Marshal Service; FBI; HHS Office of Inspector General; U.S. Immigration and Customs Enforcement; U.S. Marshals Service; and USSS—provided force protection for deployed Federal assets (e.g., FEMA US&R Task Forces) and state operations.

However, ESF #13 does not have a single, centralized source of law enforcement resources to draw from and must rely on individual ad hoc requests to Federal agencies for resources. To date, a large-scale activation of Federal public safety and security resources under ESF #13 has never occurred. While numerous full-time Federal law enforcement officers have arrest and firearm authority, not all possess wide Federal jurisdiction. As a result, many responding officers must receive special deputation by the U.S. Marshals Service. ESF #13 is currently developing the concept of alert teams, which would facilitate identification of deployable resources and help expedite their deployment. Additionally, efforts are underway to commit each partner agency to a level of resources that it will provide in a large-scale response scenario. These mechanisms will reduce uncertainty in resource availability and formalize processes for requesting resources.

Delegation and allocation of state policing authorities for Federal law enforcement officers remain varied among jurisdictions and, in some cases, are not addressed by state or local ordinance or statute. In those jurisdictions, no legal mechanism or authority exists through which Federal law enforcement officers can enforce state criminal provisions, potentially limiting the ability of these officers to assist with general policing operations. Past events demonstrate that EMAC remains the best option for a state to obtain law enforcement resources that are appropriately equipped, trained, and experienced in the enforcement of state and local laws.

Preparedness Case Study: Response to Mass Shooting Event in Minneapolis

Over the past two years, the Minneapolis Police Department and first responders in the area have participated in an integrated training program called 3 ECHO to enhance their coordination during an active shooter response. On September 27, 2012, this training was put to the test when the Minneapolis Police Department responded to a mass shooting taking place inside a business. Initial responding officers entered the building to stop the potential threat, identified the locations of survivors, and created a secure corridor for emergency medical personnel to enter so they could provide early medical intervention and evacuate injured survivors. Police, fire, and EMS personnel worked in close coordination to extract survivors quickly, while Special Weapons and Tactics personnel systematically cleared the building. All injured survivors were either at or en route to a medical facility within 24 minutes of the first call for help.

State and Territorial Preparedness Perspectives: On-scene Security and Protection

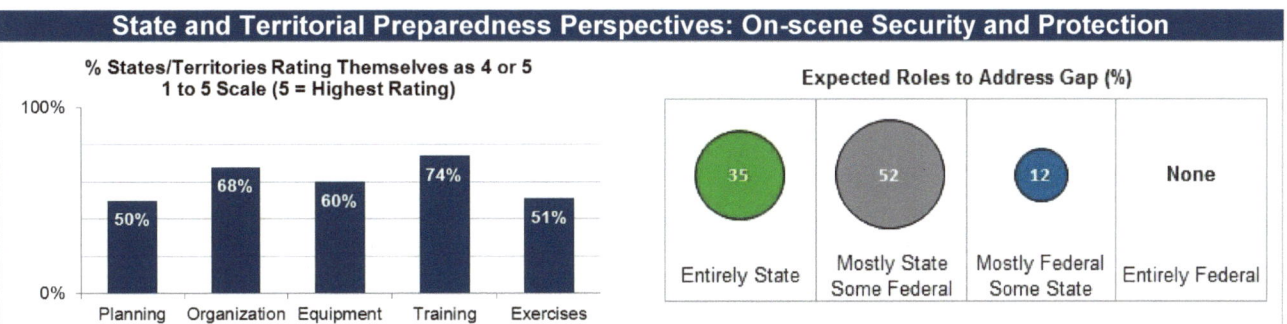

% States/Territories Rating Themselves as 4 or 5
1 to 5 Scale (5 = Highest Rating)

Planning	Organization	Equipment	Training	Exercises
50%	68%	60%	74%	51%

Expected Roles to Address Gap (%)

Entirely State	Mostly State Some Federal	Mostly Federal Some State	Entirely Federal
35	52	12	None

Operational Communications

The 2012 NPR focused on major accomplishments in strategic and tactical communications planning nationwide and on the growth in resources to support rapid restoration of communications infrastructure. In 2012, interoperability advances continued across the country, as did progress in developing a new public safety broadband network. Current NPR findings provide a status update on interoperable communications and on progress toward implementing Next Generation 9-1-1.

Key Finding: *Most counties have established capabilities to provide response-level interoperable communications within one hour of an incident.*

The *National Emergency Communications Plan* (NECP) establishes the Nation's strategic approach to improve interoperability. As a result of NECP implementation, by 2011, 90 percent of more than 2,800 counties and county-level equivalents demonstrated response-level emergency communications (i.e., managing resources and making timely decisions without technical or procedural issues impeding communications) within one hour for routine events involving multiple jurisdictions and agencies. Nationwide performance exceeds the target of 75 percent established in the NECP. In addition, DHS assessed the same counties and county-level equivalents based on the five elements of the SAFECOM Interoperability Continuum: governance; policies, practices, and procedures; technology; training and exercises; and usage. Figure 16 shows that the vast majority of counties across the country have progressed beyond the early stage of development for interoperable communications.

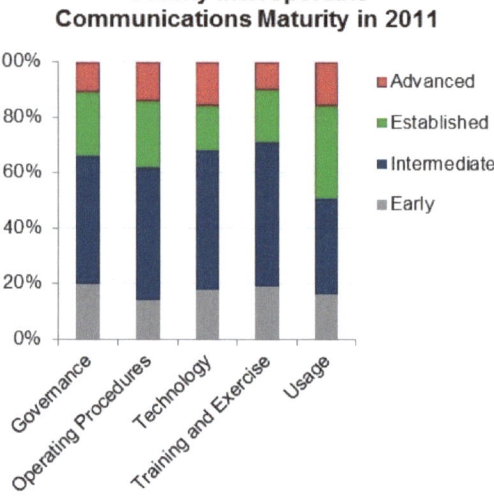

These gains have occurred, in part, due to substantial investments that have helped close numerous communications capability gaps. For example, compared with a decade ago, roughly 7,000 additional fire departments now possess sufficient radios for all shift responders—reflecting an increase of over one-fifth of all fire departments. From FY 2006 to FY 2011, state, local, tribal, and territorial governments have made investments in communications assets totaling over $3.4 billion in Federal grant funds alone. Moreover, NIST and the DHS Science and Technology Directorate continue to support research to improve radio performance, including efforts to enhance radio durability and mitigate challenges from building construction, obstructions, and other equipment. Additionally,

Figure 16: In all areas, more than 80 percent of counties have progressed beyond early-stage development of interoperable communications.

the National Fire Protection Association is developing a new performance standard for land mobile radios for emergency services personnel.

Key Finding: *Next Generation 9-1-1 (NG911) systems continue to develop, providing advanced public safety communication that allows for text and data transfer.*

Existing 9-1-1 systems support calls requesting emergency assistance, but generally do not support sending text messages, video, or photos directly to emergency authorities. To address this gap, the FCC announced a five-step plan in August 2011 to further the development and deployment of NG911—an internet protocol-based 9-1-1 system for emergency services that enables transmission of digital information from callers. In addition, the Next Generation 9-1-1 Advancement Act of 2012 requires the FCC to submit a report to Congress that provides recommendations on a legal and regulatory framework for the development of NG911 services and the transition from legacy 9-1-1 to NG911. It also establishes an office within the National Highway Traffic Safety Administration to coordinate 9-1-1 services and facilitate grant programs. Moreover, the act authorizes $115 million in grant funding for implementing 9-1-1 services.

Progress has occurred in each area of the FCC's five-step plan, which addresses developing mechanisms for location accuracy; enabling consumers to send text, photos, and video; developing a funding model for NG911; facilitating the completion and implementation of technical standards; and working with states and other stakeholders to develop a governance framework. For example, trials of text-to-9-1-1 technology are under way in Iowa, North Carolina, and Vermont. Moreover, in December 2012, the Nation's four largest wireless providers voluntarily committed to provide text-to-9-1-1 availability nationwide by May 2014. Furthermore, the FCC has proposed rules that require all wireless carriers and providers of text-messaging applications to support text-to-9-1-1 in all areas where call centers are prepared to receive texts. This new technology will enable communication in situations where a voice call could endanger the caller, or for individuals who are deaf or hard of hearing, as well as for people who may have a speech or communication disability.

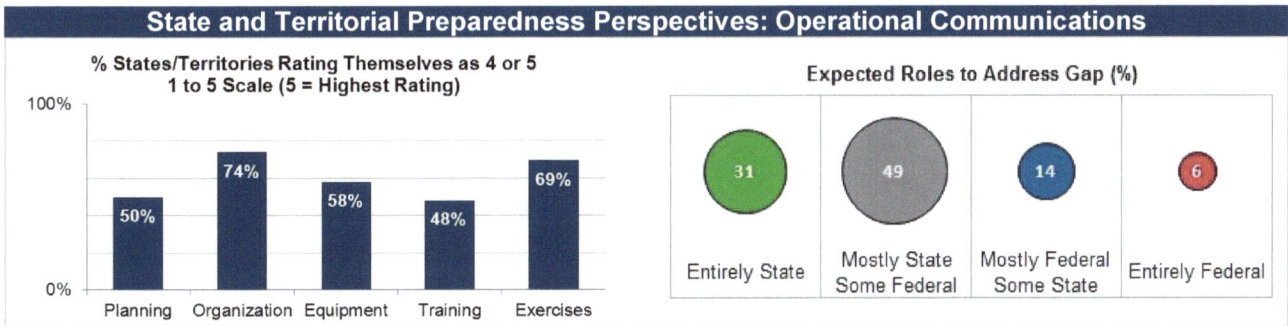

State and Territorial Preparedness Perspectives: Operational Communications

% States/Territories Rating Themselves as 4 or 5
1 to 5 Scale (5 = Highest Rating)

Planning 50% | Organization 74% | Equipment 58% | Training 48% | Exercises 69%

Expected Roles to Address Gap (%)

Entirely State 31 | Mostly State Some Federal 49 | Mostly Federal Some State 14 | Entirely Federal 6

Public and Private Services and Resources

The 2012 NPR focused on the capacity of public and private partners to provide commodity support for a major earthquake scenario, and highlighted mature fire service capabilities nationally. Current NPR findings offer additional data on public and private contributions based on Sandy, while broadening the analysis to cover existing public-private partnerships. In addition, this report explores recent developments in the Nation's strategic approach to wildfires.

Key Finding: *Public and private partners demonstrated their ability to deliver needed commodities and resources to survivors during the Sandy response.*

A network of standing arrangements with public and private partners—including interagency agreements, memoranda of understanding/agreement, contracts, and mission assignments—provides items that ESF #7 (Logistics Management and Resource Support) uses for disaster support. In the aftermath of Sandy, ESF #7 public and private partners shipped 16 million meals, 20 million liters of water, 138,000 tarps, and 570 generators. Examples of specific public and private contributions include the following:

- Prior to Sandy's arrival, FEMA and its partners pre-staged commodities and equipment, including over 461,000 meals, 892,000 liters of water, 4,200 cots, and 183 generators.

- By the ninth day after Sandy's landfall, the DOD Defense Logistics Agency (DLA) had provided more than 6.2 million meals to areas in New York and New Jersey.

- The USACE installed approximately 200 generators at hospitals, water treatment plants, high-rise buildings, and other facilities, including the Kinder Morgan Petroleum Terminal.

- To supplement New Jersey Transit Authority service in affected areas, GSA secured 220 buses, which provided rides to 126,500 survivors from November 13 to December 3, 2013. GSA also provided 600,000 blankets during the response.

Key Finding: *Ensuring the availability of fuel remains an area for improvement based on experiences during Sandy.*

Sandy revealed challenges to the Nation's ability to provide fuel in disaster-affected areas. Early in the response, since nearly all gas stations in New York City did not possess a backup generator, loss of electricity prevented them from dispensing gasoline. Meanwhile, the storm's scale disrupted the gasoline supply chain, damaging two of the region's six refineries and knocking out power to critical pipelines. More than one week after Sandy made landfall, 21 percent of gas stations across New York City did not have gas available (see Figure 17). Federal agencies supplemented fuel from the private sector by expediting the delivery of additional gasoline, diesel, and home heating oil. For example, the DOD DLA delivered 1.1 million gallons of gasoline and 333,000 gallons of diesel fuel to New York and New Jersey from October 29 to November 7. The President also directed DLA to purchase up to 12 million gallons of unleaded fuel and up to 10 million gallons of diesel fuel, and authorized an emergency diesel fuel loan from DOE's Northeast Home Heating Oil Reserve for the first time in history. While overall supplies of fuel were sufficient, inadequate visibility on gas stations in need of fuel or power, as well as inconsistent guidance on where to send the fuel, hindered distribution efforts and resulted in localized fuel shortages.

Key Finding: *Despite nationwide progress incorporating the private sector into response efforts, many public-private partnerships in emergency preparedness face challenges with respect to adequate resourcing and long-term sustainability.*

Public-private partnerships for emergency preparedness continue to mature as they seek to integrate into disaster planning and response efforts. In 2011, the National Incident Management Systems and Advanced Technologies Institute evaluated 79 different public-private partnerships against criteria in five categories: public accessibility; dedicated personnel; resourcing; engagement of leadership and members; and sustainability.[24] Only 35 percent of these partnerships satisfied all five criteria, with resourcing and sustainability of the partnerships representing the largest areas for improvement.

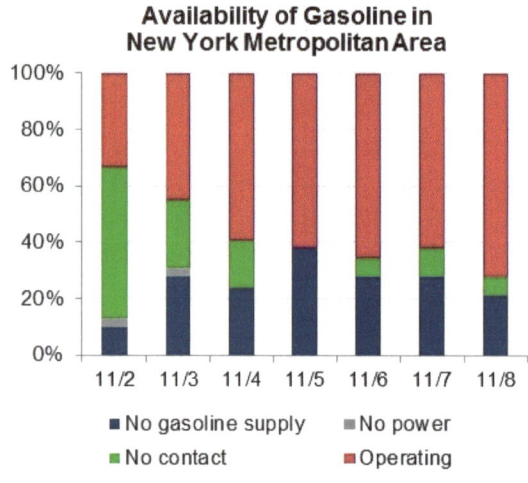

Figure 17: More than one week after Sandy, disruptions to the supply chain for gasoline persisted.

To close existing gaps, DHS highlighted private-sector engagement in preparedness grant guidance beginning in FY 2011, identifying ways states can use grant funding to support public-private collaboration. In addition, DHS increased private-sector collaboration by placing Regional Private Sector Liaisons in each of the 10 FEMA Regions and encouraging inclusion of private-sector representatives in preparedness activities. In July 2012, FEMA opened the National Business Emergency Operations Center, which serves as a virtual clearinghouse for two-way information sharing between businesses and FEMA. As of January 2013, 300 businesses had signed agreements with FEMA to share information through the virtual center, which activated during Sandy.

Key Finding: *Extensive Federal, state, and local resources are available nationally to respond to large wildfires. Rising costs and resource demands from larger, more complex fires have motivated the development of a more comprehensive wildfire management strategy that includes mitigation activities.*

In summer 2012, Colorado experienced unprecedented destruction from wildfires; for example, the Waldo Canyon Fire scorched 18,947 acres and destroyed 346 homes. Despite these and other large fires, wildland firefighting resources were not depleted. Interagency wildland firefighting resources—including more than 15,000 USDA Forest Service and U.S. Department of the Interior firefighters; interagency Incident Management Teams; and extensive aviation assets, such as helicopters and airtankers—can move anywhere in the Nation within 24 to 48 hours.

Despite this capacity, a broader strategy for wildfire management remains important. Persistent drought, fuel accumulation, and expanding development have resulted in larger, more complex fires, stressing fire suppression capabilities and increasing costs. From January to October 2012, wildfires destroyed almost 9.2 million acres of land—the third largest one-year total on record. Annual expenditures to suppress wildland fires (adjusted for inflation to 2012 dollars) have increased from an average of $416 million per year in the 1970s to an average of nearly $1.3 billion dollars in the last 10 years. To address this need, the intergovernmental Wildland Fire Leadership Council is implementing the *National Cohesive Wildland Fire Management Strategy*. The strategy focuses on enhancing wildfire response capabilities and implementing mitigation measures, such as making communities more resistant to wildfires and restoring and maintaining resilient landscapes. In addition, in December 2012, NIST and USFS released the Wildland-Urban Interface Fire Exposure Scale, which provides a framework for technically-based building codes and standards for structures located in the wildland-urban interface (i.e., where developed and undeveloped areas meet).

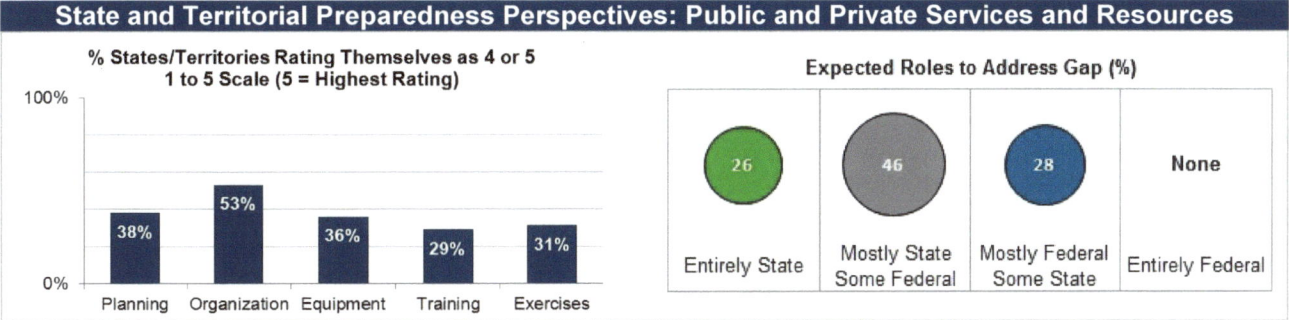

Public Health and Medical Services

The 2012 NPR detailed Federal and volunteer medical assets—including National Disaster Medical System (NDMS) teams and U.S. Public Health Service teams—that supplement state, local, tribal, and territorial public health and medical capabilities. Additional findings from that report explored medical countermeasures and the role assistance programs play in enhancing state and local capacity. Current NPR findings focus on recent accomplishments related to NDMS deployment times, medical countermeasures, challenges in sustaining public health and medical capabilities, and gaps in nursing home preparedness.

Key finding: *HHS surged NDMS resources to Sandy survivors in record time and quantities.*

In advance of Sandy's landfall, HHS relocated NDMS personnel and equipment to safe locations. By the time the storm came ashore, HHS already had teams stationed in the Northeast, with additional support arriving in the days that followed. In total, HHS deployed over 1,900 response personnel and 15 Disaster Medical Assistance Team (DMAT) equipment caches, ultimately dispatching more equipment and personnel in a shorter time than any other response in NDMS history. Historically, the standard timeframe for deploying NDMS resources has been 24 to 48 hours. However, HHS ASPR has improved the flexibility of its NDMS response capabilities to surge appropriately sized teams and medical support equipment to the field. For example, during the Sandy response, two DMATs arrived onsite in New York within 4 hours, well-ahead of the requested 12-hour window.

Key finding: *New investments in research centers, expanded countermeasure development and acquisition, and increasingly capable response assets have improved the Nation's ability to respond to a range of CBRN, pandemic flu, and emerging infectious disease threats.*

HHS is leading efforts to improve the coordination of medical countermeasure efforts across the Federal Government through the Public Health Emergency Medical Countermeasures Enterprise (PHEMCE). One component of PHEMCE is the HHS Biomedical Advanced Research and Development Authority (BARDA), which manages over 150 active contracts for the advanced development of medical countermeasures to address CBRN threats and pandemic influenza. Since 2007, this deep pipeline has delivered or is nearing delivery of seven new critical medical countermeasures to be added to the Strategic National Stockpile. In addition, in 2012, BARDA supported development of the first cell-based influenza vaccine to receive licensure in the United States, ultimately helping to reduce response times during an influenza pandemic. In 2012, BARDA also established three Centers for Innovation in Advanced Development and Manufacturing, which are new public-private partnerships that enable rapid production of medical countermeasures to protect the public from bioterrorism, pandemic influenza, and other epidemics. The partnerships combine innovative ideas from small biotech firms, the training expertise of academic institutions, and the development and manufacturing experience of large pharmaceutical companies. In 2012, DOD finalized source selection for an advanced development capability for medical countermeasures to complement the HHS centers, focusing on DOD warfighter needs and—by extension—public health needs.

HHS continued to document state and local capabilities to conduct medical countermeasure planning through CDC's Technical Assistance Review process, which evaluates state and local plans to request, receive, distribute, and dispense medical countermeasures. These reviews assess plans on a scale of 0 to 100. Figure 18 shows that state scores trended upward from 2007 to 2012. To address lingering challenges in implementing these plans, CDC's Cities Readiness Initiative (CRI) helps communities

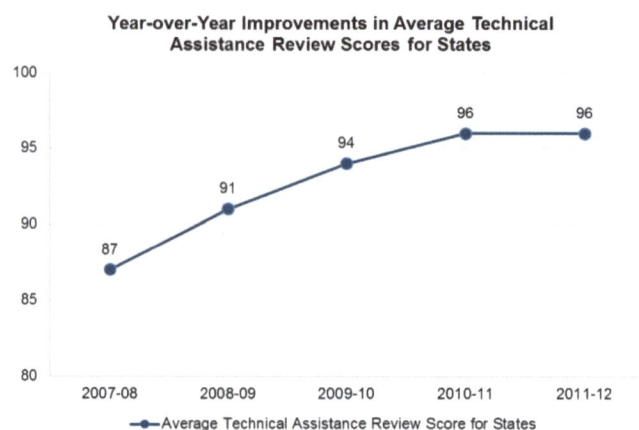

Figure 18: CDC cooperative agreements supported steady improvements to state plans for receiving and distributing medical countermeasures.

to develop alternative medical countermeasure distribution and dispensing solutions using local employers, community strike teams, community-based organizations, and the U.S. Postal Service (USPS). First piloted in 2004 in 21 jurisdictions, CRI encompassed 72 metropolitan areas as of 2012, covering nearly 60 percent of the U.S. population.

Preparedness Case Study: Local Distribution of Medical Countermeasures

In May 2012, HHS sponsored a full-scale exercise in Minneapolis and St. Paul, Minnesota, to test the National Postal Model. Under this approach, USPS resources help distribute medical countermeasures to the public in a public health emergency. This model supplements mass dispensing sites and other distribution methods in place locally across the Nation. In the first full-scale exercise of the National Postal Model, participating local and state agencies and non-governmental organizations successfully collaborated with their Federal partners to deliver simulated antibiotic supplies to over 95 percent of nearly 35,000 residential mailing addresses across four different ZIP codes within nine hours—using fewer than 40 teams of letter carriers and law enforcement personnel. Some of the lessons learned are shaping similar mass prophylaxis planning efforts elsewhere, and are improving preparedness for a pandemic, anthrax attack, or other public health emergency.

Key finding: *While some public health and medical response capabilities continue to improve, reductions in public health funding and personnel could affect recent progress.*

Recent program performance data and annual studies related to public health confirm that the Nation has made strides in preparedness planning and coordination; medical countermeasure development, manufacturing, and distribution; and some public health response capabilities. For example, the HHS Hospital Preparedness Program has awarded over $4 billion to states, territories, and large metropolitan areas since 2002 to improve preparedness of healthcare systems nationwide. As Figure 19 shows, overall HPP performance has improved since 2011. The development of healthcare coalitions remains an area of focus for the program. All HPP-funded

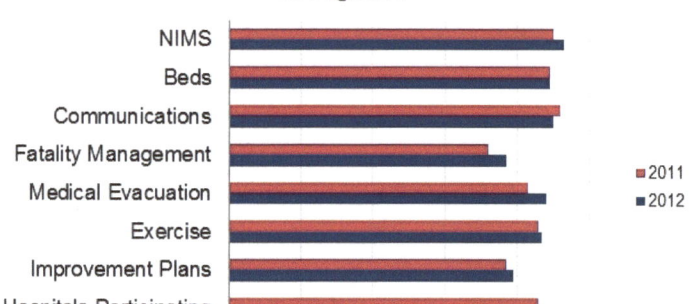

Figure 19: HPP has strengthened healthcare systems' overall capacity to respond to disasters, as well as their overall resilience.

states, localities, and territories can report data on available beds within four hours of a request, and 88 percent of participating hospitals can report data on available beds to state emergency operations centers within 60 minutes. In addition, a 2012 state-by-state study by the CDC reported continued progress in public health preparedness activities.

Continued job losses and funding cuts at state and local health departments, coupled with uncertainty in Federal funding could stall recent progress. From FY 2010 to FY 2012, 29 states cut funding for public health programs, and 23 states cut health budgets two or more years in a row. The Association of State and Territorial Health Officials reports that state and local health departments have cut more than 45,700 jobs across the country since 2008.[25] In 2010, 47 states reported having sufficient public health laboratory staff capacity to work five, 12-hour days for six to eight weeks in response to an infectious disease outbreak, such as novel influenza A H1N1.[26] By 2012, only 37 states and the District of Columbia reported having similar capacity.[27]

Key finding: *While a large majority of nursing homes met Federal emergency planning and preparedness requirements in 2011, experiences during recent disasters indicate that many nursing homes may not be as prepared as these figures suggest.*

Federal regulations require that nursing homes have plans and procedures in place to respond to emergencies, train employees on those guidelines, and periodically review and test them through drills. Before Hurricane Katrina in 2005, 94 percent of certified facilities met Federal standards for emergency plans and 80 percent of staff met emergency training requirements, despite the widespread deficiencies exposed during the 2005 response. As of March 2011, 92 percent of nursing homes reported addressing emergency plan provisions and 72 percent met training thresholds.

However, in 2012, HHS released a report that evaluated 24 nursing homes in seven states affected by disasters from 2007 to 2010. Results indicate that nursing home facilities may not be as prepared as those results indicate. While the evaluation did not include a nationally representative sample, it found that 17 of the 24 nursing homes surveyed reported substantial challenges during response and recovery efforts. These challenges included information gaps in emergency plans; a lack of collaboration with emergency management; unreliable transportation contracts; and difficultly tracking residents between evacuating and receiving nursing homes. More recently, following Sandy, reports emerged of nursing homes experiencing difficulties with patient evacuation, backup generators, family notification, adequate food and medical supplies, and medical records.[28,29] HHS continues to promote nursing home participation in emergency planning and preparedness efforts. For example, in 2012, HPP identified these types of facilities as an essential partner in healthcare coalitions, promoted their participation in training and exercises, and required program awardees to participate emergency planning concerning individuals with special medical needs.

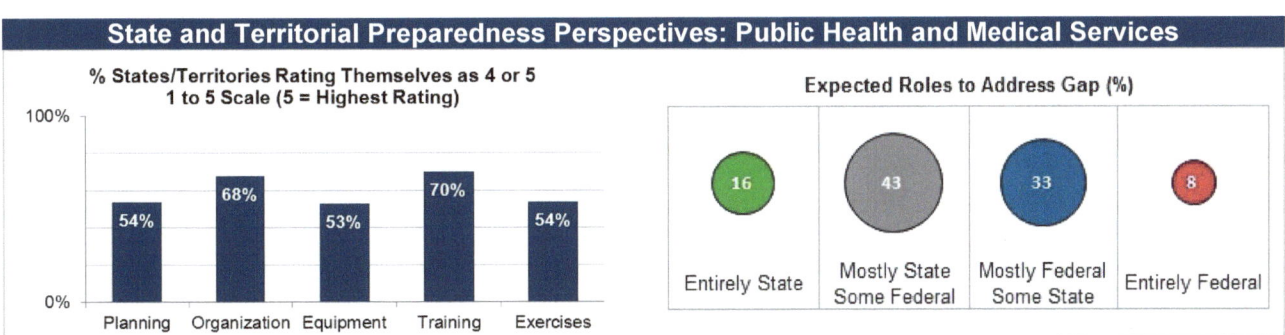

State and Territorial Preparedness Perspectives: Public Health and Medical Services

% States/Territories Rating Themselves as 4 or 5
1 to 5 Scale (5 = Highest Rating)

Planning 54% · Organization 68% · Equipment 53% · Training 70% · Exercises 54%

Expected Roles to Address Gap (%)

Entirely State 16 · Mostly State Some Federal 43 · Mostly Federal Some State 33 · Entirely Federal 8

Situational Assessment

The 2012 NPR noted the growth of social media and geographical information systems nationally and cited these platforms as valuable situational awareness tools. The current NPR explores how emergency management agencies are using geospatial and social media information to enhance response and recovery operations.

Key Finding: *Adoption of crisis information management systems and ongoing data integration efforts have improved real-time information sharing and situational awareness.*

An increasing number of emergency operation centers have turned to crisis management software to improve the flow of disaster-related information. For example, over the past two years, DOT has used commercial web-enabled software for incident and event management to enhance its ability to transfer real-time, transportation-related information to the National Response Coordination Center (NRCC), Regional Response Coordination Centers, and Joint Field Offices, facilitating the rapid transport of response teams and commodities into affected areas. In August 2012, FEMA began using the same system, in part to eliminate the need to access multiple systems with separate user names and passwords.

Response and recovery efforts following Sandy confirmed challenges associated with establishing shared, real-time situational awareness across levels of government and among whole community partners. Seamless data-sharing among Federal, state, and local agencies remains the goal, including for agencies using the same type of crisis management software. At the Federal level, DOT plans to integrate its information status boards into FEMA's system to improve coordination between both agencies. Similarly, some states plan to link local emergency operation centers to their state emergency operations center to facilitate the rapid exchange of essential information.

Efforts are not limited to incident management software. Agencies have also explored integrating other real-time data streams, often in geographic information system (GIS) formats. During Hurricane Isaac, DOT coordinated with state partners to incorporate real-time traffic information systems (i.e., 5-1-1 systems) into FEMA's GIS interface. Additionally, personnel from 12 Federal agencies and selected electric industry representatives have access to DOE's in-house monitoring and mapping GIS tool, EAGLE-I. The system provides near real-time information regarding the Nation's energy grids and networks and is now displayed in Federal operations centers at DOE, DHS, HHS, DOD, USDA, and the National Weather Service, following its security certification in November 2012. FEMA also has coordinated with over 20 private sector businesses to map real-time information on the operating status of retail locations and distribution centers, helping the Agency to source relief commodities locally and scale back relief operations when businesses have reopened post-disaster. Most recently, *PPD-21: Critical Infrastructure and Resilience*, released in February 2013, requires DHS to achieve a near real-time situational awareness capability for critical infrastructure, including dissemination of critical information to save or sustain lives, mitigate damage, or reduce further degradation during an incident.

Key Finding: *Emergency management agencies are increasingly using social media to disseminate information and are exploring additional applications of social media.*

The role of social media in disaster response continues to evolve. In a 2012 American Red Cross telephone survey of over 1,000 people, 70 percent of respondents agreed that emergency response agencies should regularly monitor their websites and social media sites so that personnel can respond promptly to any posted requests for help.[30] Correspondingly, 77 percent of respondents to a 2012 nationwide survey of 504 state and local emergency management agencies indicated that their agency uses social media, with 55 percent setting the goal of monitoring social media information posted during an event.[31] At the Federal level, FEMA has expanded social media monitoring at watch centers such as the NRCC. The CDC also uses social media to share guidance on health protection measures before and after disasters.

A 2011 FEMA assessment of NRCC activities during Hurricane Irene uncovered a lack of clarity among NRCC personnel in how they should use social media. One challenge is that social media data come from unofficial sources, presenting issues with data verification and reliability that affect how decision-makers can use that information. Thus, most emergency management agencies use social media primarily to push information to the public. For example, after Sandy, FEMA established a "Rumor Control" website to counter misinformation spread through social media. Moreover, FEMA used crowdsourcing to conduct an initial review and provide basic damage assessment using numerous aerial images of the affected areas taken by the Civil Air Patrol. In addition, FEMA used its smartphone application to show the locations of open shelters and Disaster Recovery Centers and to help people apply online for disaster assistance.

Key Finding: *By combining and visualizing data inputs in geospatial formats, responders have improved situational awareness of severely impacted areas and accelerated resource-allocation decisions.*

The devastation caused by Sandy left many areas that required housing assistance inaccessible, due to road blockages and flooding. These obstacles made traditional on-site damage assessments impossible. Thus, FEMA turned to geospatial technology to expedite over $130 million in rental assistance funds to over 44,000 disaster survivors. Specifically, FEMA's Modeling Task Force used several sources of data, including: storm surge forecast models from the National Hurricane Center's Sea, Lake, and Overland Surges from Hurricanes (SLOSH) model; USGS field observations of storm surge flood depths; imagery data from the Civil

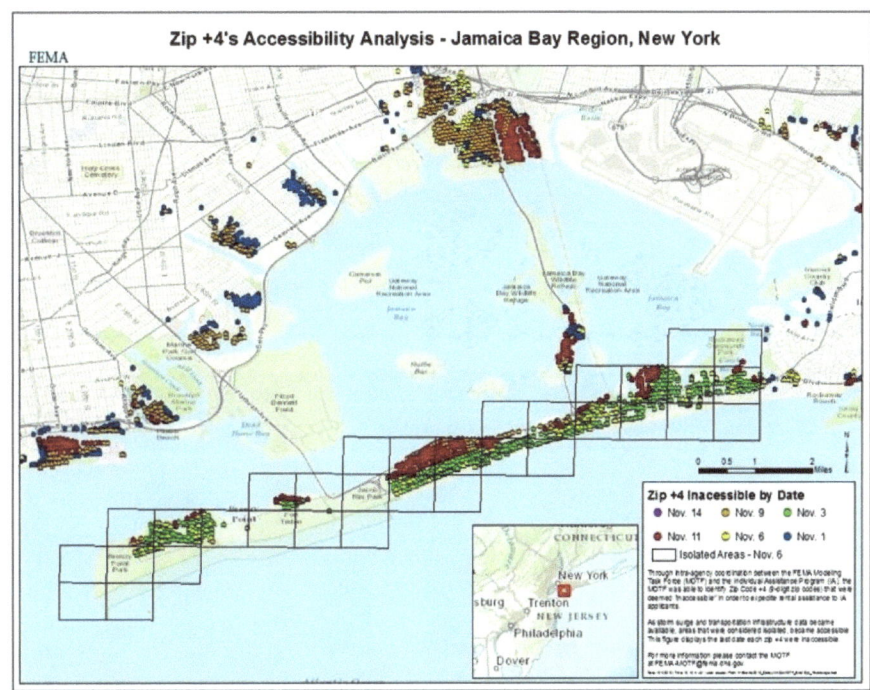

Figure 20: Within three days of Sandy's arrival, FEMA's Modeling Task Force created GIS products that mapped areas eligible for expedited rental assistance.

Air Patrol, NOAA, and Customs and Border Protection; and road closure data. The team used these inputs to create and update geospatial analyses identifying "zip code + 4" areas that were likely inaccessible (see Figure 20). The expedited rental assistance allowed survivors to relocate while waiting for their homes to become accessible again to start the on-the-ground inspection process. Eligible applicants in these areas automatically qualified for two months of expedited rental assistance.

Preparedness Case Study: Real-time App Modifications Support Disaster Survivors

Numerous response organizations have developed smartphone applications (or "apps") to disseminate information rapidly to survivors and disaster workers. Among those used during Sandy response and recovery was the American Red Cross hurricane app (see Figure 21), which helped users to track the storm; locate shelter; and access safety tips about mold, downed electrical wires, and safe generator use. Users downloaded the American Red Cross hurricane app 400,000 times in the aftermath of Sandy. Despite widespread power and mobile telephone outages after the storm, smartphone apps delivered valuable real-time information to survivors.

Figure 21: The American Red Cross hurricane app delivered real-time information about available resources to disaster survivors after Sandy.

State and Territorial Preparedness Perspectives: Situational Assessment

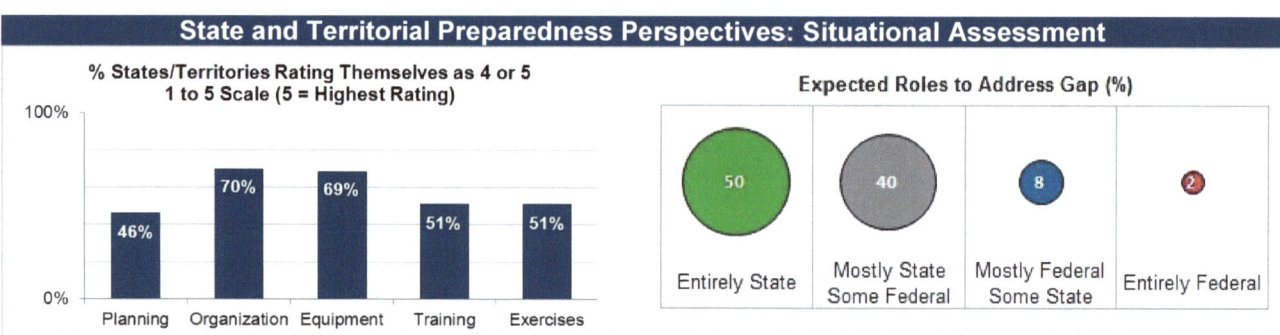

% States/Territories Rating Themselves as 4 or 5
1 to 5 Scale (5 = Highest Rating)

- Planning: 46%
- Organization: 70%
- Equipment: 69%
- Training: 51%
- Exercises: 51%

Expected Roles to Address Gap (%)

- Entirely State: 50
- Mostly State Some Federal: 40
- Mostly Federal Some State: 8
- Entirely Federal: 2

Response/Recovery Core Capabilities

Infrastructure Systems

Post-disaster stabilization and restoration of critical infrastructure are vital to post-disaster recovery operations. The 2012 NPR highlighted proven infrastructure mutual aid networks, but noted that long-term infrastructure recovery capabilities are in the early stages of development. The current NPR finding focuses on the links between infrastructure systems and disaster response and recovery efforts.

Key finding: *Stressed infrastructure across the country may affect the Nation's ability to respond to and recover from a disaster.*

As of December 2012, the Federal Highway Administration's National Bridge Inventory notes that approximately 25 percent of the Nation's bridges are either structurally deficient or functionally obsolete. The American Society of Civil Engineers (ASCE) reports that aging wastewater systems release approximately 900 billion gallons of untreated sewage every year.[32] The age, design, and condition of infrastructure can worsen the effects of disasters. For example, in fall 2012, Sandy damaged infrastructure, resulting in protracted power outages and extensive damage to transportation assets. Climate change and extreme weather events also expose vulnerabilities in key infrastructure sectors—including transportation and commercial facilities.

The Nation is making targeted progress in maintaining and improving its infrastructure. For example, large-scale infrastructure investments—such as the Next Generation Air Transportation System, the Smart Grid Investment Grants, and the Hurricane and Storm Damage Risk Reduction System in New Orleans—have funded improvements in key facets of the Nation's infrastructure. In addition, in December 2012, the Federal Highway Administration released a vulnerability assessment framework to help organizations analyze the effects of climate change and extreme weather on transportation infrastructure. This tool reflects lessons from recent pilot projects in Washington, Virginia, New Jersey, Hawaii, and California. Despite these efforts, gaps remain in infrastructure resources. Based on current investment trends, the ASCE estimated a $1.1 trillion funding gap by 2020 for the Nation's water and wastewater treatment; surface transportation; airports; inland waterways and marine ports; and electricity infrastructures.[33]

Preparedness Case Study: Real-time Crisis Mapping During Sandy

Students at Franklin High School in New Brunswick, NJ used an online mapping service to publish information on gas stations in the area, noting whether they were open, had power, had available fuel, and/or served as charging stations. Students gathered information from personal observations, direct contact with gas stations, media reports, and updates from social media outlets such as Twitter and Facebook. The students created a map outlining the status of fuel resources in the community. The information then fed directly into an open, online crisis response platform, allowing thousands of people to access the information. This updated information reduced wait times for drivers seeking to refuel and helped government and commercial partners to direct power and fuel resources to the most affected areas.

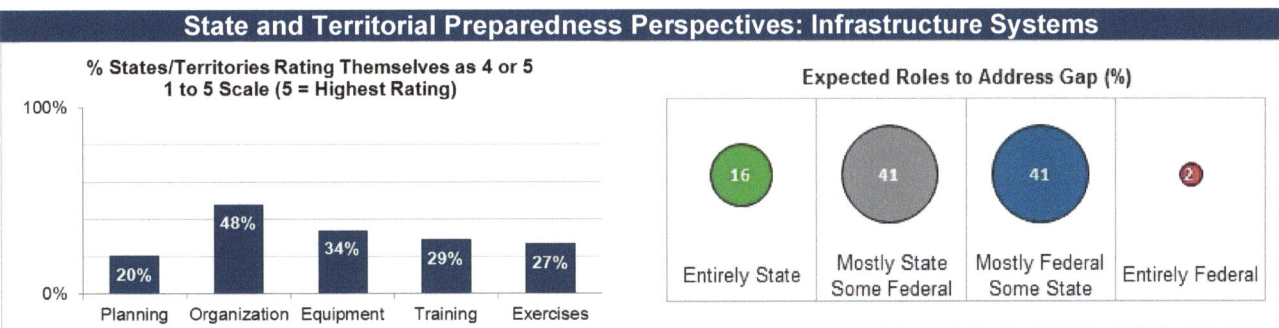

State and Territorial Preparedness Perspectives: Infrastructure Systems

% States/Territories Rating Themselves as 4 or 5
1 to 5 Scale (5 = Highest Rating)

Planning 20% · Organization 48% · Equipment 34% · Training 29% · Exercises 27%

Expected Roles to Address Gap (%)

Entirely State 16 · Mostly State Some Federal 41 · Mostly Federal Some State 41 · Entirely Federal 2

Recovery Core Capabilities

Economic Recovery

Disasters create challenges for communities that are trying to return to normal economic and business activities in a timely fashion. The 2012 NPR addressed state efforts to foster economic recovery and the status of private sector planning for disaster recovery. The current NPR focuses on recent Federal activities to help businesses recover from disasters.

Key finding: *Federal agencies and their partners improved existing initiatives to deliver economic recovery support to businesses in response to recent disasters.*

Many businesses struggle to re-open after a disaster. Impediments to post-disaster business recovery may include decreased cash flow, minimal awareness of available relief programs, possible increased insurance costs, concerns about assuming additional debt, and lack of pre-disaster business continuity planning. To help address these challenges, in 2012, the Federal Government and whole community partners streamlined existing programs to facilitate economic recovery. For example, USDA simplified its disaster designation process and streamlined its aid applications to accelerate drought recovery. USDA and the U.S. Small Business Administration (SBA) also coordinated closely to speed availability of SBA Economic Injury Disaster Loan assistance to affected businesses. In addition, during the 2012 droughts, the 16 primary crop insurance providers waived interest charges on unpaid premiums from August through November 2012. Moreover, USDA reduced emergency loan interest rates by 1.5 percent and decreased producers' rental payments from 25 percent to 10 percent to support emergency haying and grazing on Conservation Reserve Program lands. To speed recovery after Sandy, the New York City Industrial Development Agency provided sales tax exemptions on rebuilding materials for affected businesses.[34] In addition, assets from the U.S. Customs and Border Protection Office of Air and Marine flew over 240 hours moving personnel and equipment from across the country to the affected areas to enable airports and seaports to resume operations and process cargo essential to the economy. The U.S. Department of Labor awarded $47 million in National Emergency Grants to states impacted by Sandy to temporarily employ workers on renovation, cleaning, and reconstruction projects. The Labor Department also distributed over $28 million in Disaster Unemployment Assistance for states to provide temporary financial assistance to individuals whose employment was lost or interrupted as a result of Sandy.

Preparedness Case Study: Small Business Recovery in Cedar Rapids, Iowa

In July 2008, flooding in Iowa's Cedar River affected over 1,000 businesses and triggered the loss of more than 2,500 jobs. Shortly thereafter, local business owners established the Cedar Rapids Small Business Recovery Group, which implemented three major initiatives in conjunction with the Cedar Rapids Chamber of Commerce. A case management project provided one-on-one technical support to 565 community businesses, and a working capital initiative distributed over $6 million to 330 small businesses to help them resume operations quickly. Finally, a mentorship program paired affected and non-affected businesses and offered assistance, temporary facilities, and additional resources to accelerate recovery. Through these efforts, the three-year survival rate for Cedar Rapids businesses was 82 percent.[35]

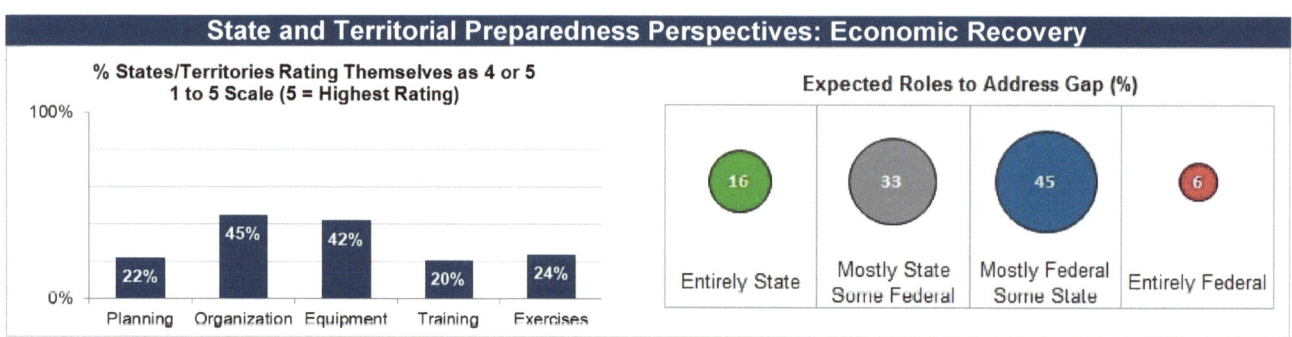

State and Territorial Preparedness Perspectives: Economic Recovery

% States/Territories Rating Themselves as 4 or 5
1 to 5 Scale (5 = Highest Rating)

Planning 22% — Organization 45% — Equipment 42% — Training 20% — Exercises 24%

Expected Roles to Address Gap (%)

Entirely State 16 — Mostly State Some Federal 33 — Mostly Federal Some State 45 — Entirely Federal 6

Health and Social Services

The 2012 NPR identified shortcomings in the integration of behavioral health concerns into recovery operations and identified the need for assessments of long-term recovery efforts for health and social services. Current NPR findings center on integrating behavioral health into recovery efforts, as well as on addressing the long-term emotional needs of children recovering from a disaster.

Key finding: *HHS made progress integrating behavioral health initiatives into disaster recovery efforts by outlining activities that address behavioral health post-disaster and studying ways to measure behavioral health recovery in affected communities.*

Since March 2011, HHS has published four strategic plans or guidance documents outlining the Department's roles, responsibilities, and key activities to support integration of behavioral health into disaster preparedness, response, and recovery efforts. These plans include the *Disaster Behavioral Health Concept of Operations*, the *Implementation Plan for the National Health Security Strategy*, *Healthcare Preparedness Capabilities* guidance for the HPP program, and the strategic plan for the Substance Abuse and Mental Health Services Administration. Through these plans, HHS has established a foundation for Federal efforts to mitigate the behavioral health effects of disasters and has improved integration with state, local, tribal, and territorial recovery activities.

HHS also launched studies to identify factors that contribute to behavioral and mental health recovery in affected communities. For instance, in 2011, HHS's National Institute of Environmental Health and Science initiated a 10-year study that is exploring the health effects of the BP Deepwater Horizon oil spill—including behavioral health—on up to 55,000 individuals who supported cleanup efforts. In 2012, the CDC initiated two research projects to examine characteristics, practices, and performance of pre- and post-disaster public health and mental health systems to identify factors that facilitate community resilience and recovery.

Key finding: *Federal programs are increasingly seeking to address the emotional impacts of disasters on children.*

Studies reviewing long-term recovery efforts of Hurricane Katrina and the BP Deepwater Horizon oil spill show that children are more susceptible to the emotional impacts of disasters than adults.[36] Moreover, children affected by disasters commonly experience challenges in school, including academic issues, behavioral problems, and absenteeism.[37] In response, the NDMS—a partnership among HHS, DOD, DHS, and the U.S. Department of Veterans Affairs serving to supplement medical response to major disasters—is training all of its personnel in psychological first aid to address the emotional and behavioral health needs of disaster responders and survivors, including children. In addition, FEMA and the National Center for Missing and Exploited Children launched a national initiative in 2012 to assist with post-disaster reunification of children with their families. The U.S. Department of Education also continued to offer psychological first aid and other recovery resources for teachers, parents, and students to address addressing psychological, emotional, and behavioral health needs after traumatic events.

Preparedness Case Study: Enhancing Local Hospital Resilience

After Susquehanna River flooding in 2006, Our Lady of Lourdes Hospital in Binghamton, New York, suffered more than $20 million in losses and had to halt critical operations for two weeks. With 16 to 20 inches of contaminated floodwater covering the hospital's ground floor, the power plant and other essential components (including emergency generators, fuel tanks, and water supply) sustained severe damage. As a result, the hospital had to relocate patients to two other area hospitals. The community used mitigation funding to repair the damage and build a floodwall, costing approximately $7 million. The reinforced concrete floodwall extends 1,365 feet around the hospital and is 14 feet tall. During Tropical Storm Lee in 2011, hospital staff successfully implemented the facility emergency plan and manually closed all 10 floodwall gates. The hospital operated at full capacity throughout the storm and experienced no flood damage.

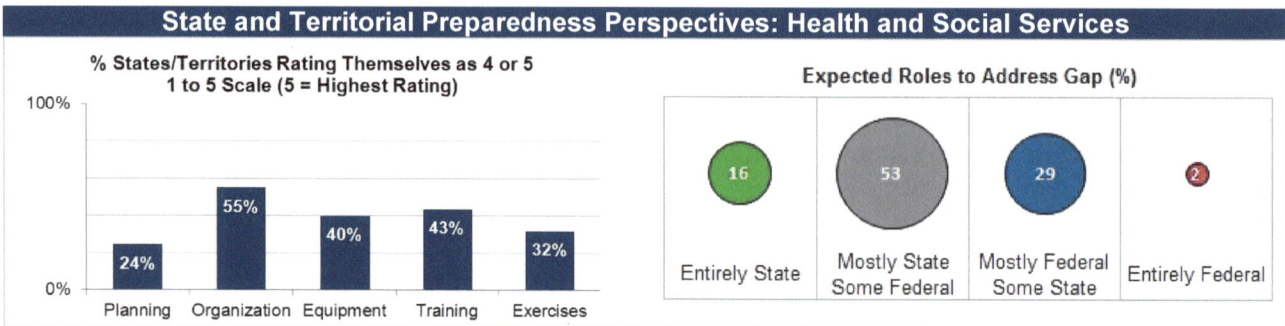

Housing

Hurricane Katrina demonstrated that the Nation was not fully prepared to provide interim and long-term housing to large numbers of displaced disaster survivors, especially those with disabilities and access and functional needs. Both the 2012 and 2013 NPRs identify improvements in this capability. Sandy further illustrated that additional work is required to provide disaster housing effectively and efficiently following a large-scale event. Moreover, 63 percent of states and territories indicated they were mostly or wholly reliant on the Federal Government for closing housing-related capability gaps, more than any other capability.

Key Finding: *FEMA's new* Catastrophic Housing Annex *serves as a guide to help state, local, tribal, and territorial governments develop plans to meet the disaster housing needs of their citizens following a catastrophic event, but coordinating the transition from shelters to interim housing remains a challenge nationally.*

FEMA released the draft *Catastrophic Housing Annex* in August 2012 as an add-on to the 2012 *Federal Interagency Response Plan–Hurricane*. The annex describes a concept of operations for transitioning 500,000 households (i.e., 1.75 million individuals with their pets and service animals) from shelters to temporary and sustainable housing. FEMA applied concepts from the draft annex following Sandy, in partnership with state-led Disaster Housing Task Forces and the NDRF Housing Recovery Support Function. Actions included increasing rental assistance to 125 percent of fair market rent, initiating a pilot program to fund short-term residential repairs to allow residents to return to or remain in their homes, staging temporary housing units for potential deployment, and renovating housing facilities at Fort Monmouth, New Jersey for use by displaced disaster survivors.

Despite these successes, Sandy demonstrated that challenges remain in addressing temporary, long-term, and permanent housing needs post-disaster. One month after the storm, shelters still housed approximately 500 individuals. To begin with, New York and New Jersey faced housing shortages even before the storm. In addition, FEMA's ability to set up temporary housing units was limited because the agency cannot place manufactured homes in high-risk flood areas (called Special Flood Hazard Areas). FEMA plans to update the annex based on lessons learned from Sandy to further detail the transition from sheltering to interim housing and expand its application to other types of disasters. In addition, the Secretary of the U.S. Department of Housing and Urban Development is leading the Federal Government's long-term Sandy recovery efforts to help address ongoing challenges with housing, economic recovery, and community redevelopment.

Key Finding: *Federal agencies are working with housing industry partners—and with accessible housing and other disability services and advocacy groups—to improve accessibility of temporary housing units.*

Nearly a quarter of Hurricane Katrina evacuees had disabilities, but only 2 percent of FEMA trailers met accessibility standards at the time.[38] Since that time, FEMA has improved efforts to provide housing for disaster survivors with access and functional needs. FEMA uses *Uniform Federal Accessibility Standards* (UFAS) requirements as a minimum standard for accessible temporary housing. In 2006, FEMA set a target to have a minimum of 5 percent of FEMA temporary housing units compliant with UFAS and, in 2012, FEMA increased this target to 15 percent. FEMA maintains contracts to procure temporary housing units as needed, with no difference in delivery timelines for standard versus UFAS-compliant units.

In addition, the Access Board—an independent Federal agency committed to addressing issues of accessibility for individuals with disabilities—is working to tailor the requirements of UFAS to account for design constraints of emergency transportable units. The proposed changes relax some UFAS technical criteria (e.g., the allowable incline of entry ramps) but strengthen other requirements (e.g., requiring folding seats in roll-in showers).[39]

Preparedness Case Study: Transforming Shipping Containers into Temporary Housing Units in New York City

In 2007, the New York City Office of Emergency Management launched the "What If New York City?" design competition for post-disaster provisional housing with support from the Rockefeller Foundation and in consultation with Architecture for Humanity-New York. The program solicited ideas and innovative solutions for disaster housing in an urban environment. In 2008, the city selected 10 winners from 117 submissions and decided to pursue stackable shipping containers as temporary housing units. Subsequent efforts have continued to create a housing solution that is deployable, reusable, cost- and energy-efficient, secure, and compliant with the Americans with Disabilities Act. Sandy recently validated the need for temporary housing solutions. The city plans to build a 16-unit prototype in 2013.

State and Territorial Preparedness Perspectives: Housing

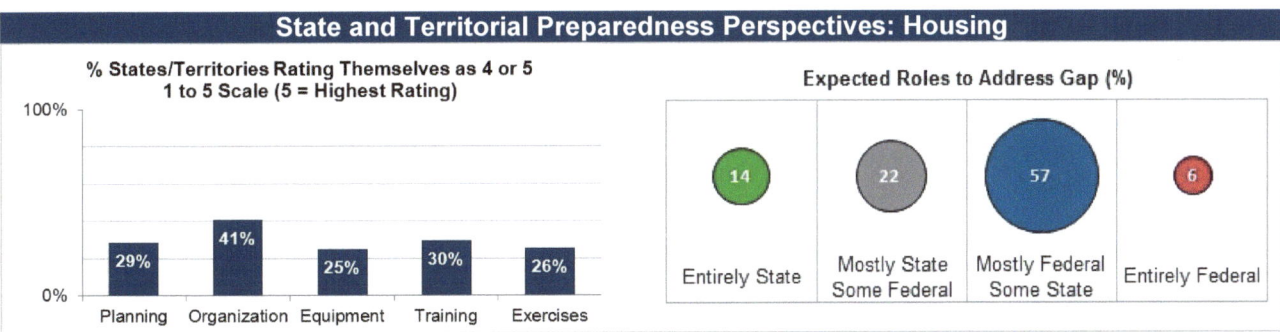

% States/Territories Rating Themselves as 4 or 5
1 to 5 Scale (5 = Highest Rating)

- Planning: 29%
- Organization: 41%
- Equipment: 25%
- Training: 30%
- Exercises: 26%

Expected Roles to Address Gap (%)

- Entirely State: 14
- Mostly State Some Federal: 22
- Mostly Federal Some State: 57
- Entirely Federal: 6

Natural and Cultural Resources

Effective recovery activities for natural and cultural resources involve pre-and post-disaster actions to preserve, conserve, rehabilitate, and restore these resources consistent with community priorities. The 2012 NPR focused on progress toward protecting vital cultural resources, specifically records management. To broaden the analysis, the current NPR focuses attention on natural resources.

Key finding: *The BP Deepwater Horizon oil spill recovery demonstrates the ability of natural resource partners to manage large-scale recovery efforts, although the spill presents long-term challenges to Gulf Coast restoration.*

In April 2010, the BP Deepwater Horizon explosion killed 11 workers and triggered the largest oil spill in U.S. history. Since 2011, natural resource partners have demonstrated their ability to effectively manage extensive recovery efforts associated with the spill. The Natural Resource Damage Assessment (NRDA) for the BP Deepwater Horizon Oil Spill is the largest ever undertaken. As of April 2012, NRDA teams surveyed more than 4,300 miles of shoreline; collected, treated, relocated, and removed affected animal species; and collected almost 50,000 samples for analysis. In addition to the activities already authorized by the Oil Pollution Act, Congress passed the 2012 Resources and Ecosystems Sustainability, Tourist Opportunities, and Revived Economy of the Gulf Coast ("RESTORE") Act, which dedicates 80 percent of potential Clean Water Act civil penalties to restoration activities benefiting the five Gulf States. The RESTORE Act represents a major investment in environmental restoration; the United States has already entered into a consent decree with Transocean that will provide for $800 million in funding under the Act, with additional claims pending. Due to the spill's unprecedented magnitude, Gulf Coast restoration is expected to challenge recovery capabilities for natural resources well into the future.

Preparedness Case Study: Providing Online Recovery Support for Cultural Resources

In 2006, the Institute of Museum and Library Services (IMLS) launched its Connecting to Collections (C2C) initiative, which emphasizes safe conditions for collections, emergency plans, accountability, and private- and public-sector collaboration in caring for the collections. In 2011, IMLS funded a free, online resource to provide smaller museums, libraries, archives, and historical societies with quick-response support for collections care and reliable preservation resources. In 2012, membership more than doubled, from approximately 900 members to over 2,000. Today, the C2C Online Community (administered by Heritage Preservation) provides online courses, discussion forums, webinars, and collections care resources, many of which emphasize emergency preparedness and disaster response. Recent additions to the online site include resources about Sandy recovery efforts.

State and Territorial Preparedness Perspectives: Natural and Cultural Resources

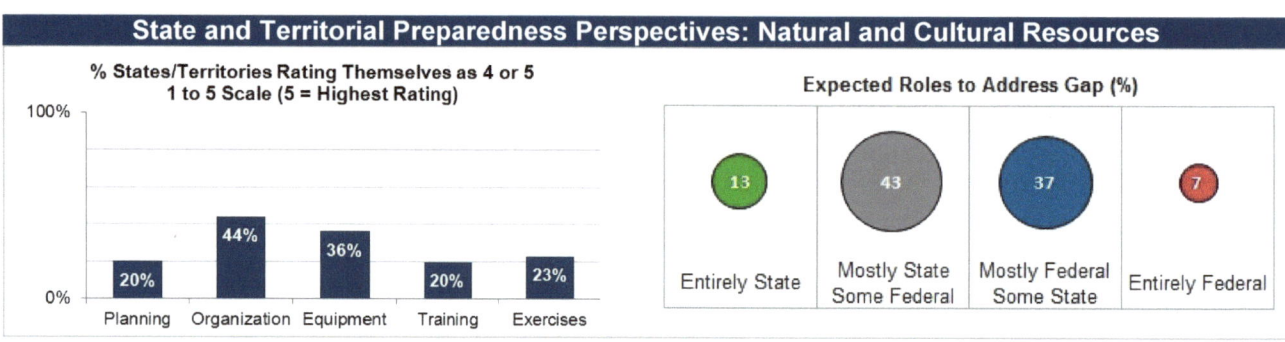

% States/Territories Rating Themselves as 4 or 5
1 to 5 Scale (5 = Highest Rating)

Planning: 20% | Organization: 44% | Equipment: 36% | Training: 20% | Exercises: 23%

Expected Roles to Address Gap (%)

Entirely State: 13 | Mostly State Some Federal: 43 | Mostly Federal Some State: 37 | Entirely Federal: 7

Conclusion

The 2013 NPR represents the second opportunity for the Nation to reflect on collective progress in building national preparedness and to identify where preparedness gaps remain. Notable developments are evident across all mission areas, including the following overarching key findings:

- The Nation continued progress in enhancing areas of national strength identified in the 2012 NPR. However, more significant changes in capability levels and overall national preparedness will become clearer by evaluating trends across multiple years.

- The Nation has made important progress in the national areas for improvement identified in the 2012 NPR, but challenges remain.

- Enhancing the resilience of infrastructure systems and maturing the role of public-private partnerships are newly identified national areas for improvement.

- Sandy response and recovery efforts highlighted strengths in the Nation's ability to expedite resources, develop innovative solutions to meet survivor needs, and work with nongovernmental partners. However, challenges remain with the Federal Government's ability to coordinate efforts when surging resources to respond to disasters

- States and territories continue to report the highest capability levels in those areas frequently cited as high priority. Interstate mutual aid plays a limited role in augmenting the capabilities of states and territories.

- In areas where current capability continues to lag, many states and territories do not expect to build additional capacity and intend to rely on Federal assets to close existing gaps.

- Whole community partners continue to use preparedness assistance programs to maintain capability strengths and address identified gaps, while key Federal sponsors are identifying strategies to improve program effectiveness and efficiency.

- Resilience initiatives are improving the Nation's ability to measure how well communities can prepare for and adapt to changing conditions, and withstand and recover rapidly from disruptions.

Each year, the Nation makes additional advances toward realizing the *National Preparedness Goal* and implementing the National Preparedness System through improved guidance and new partnerships involving all levels of government; private and nonprofit sectors; faith-based organizations; communities; and individuals. This year, the THIRA process introduced new approaches to identifying and assessing risk from the local, state, and regional perspectives, while state and territorial capability assessments shed light on the expected role that the Federal Government will play in addressing identified gaps. Ongoing national planning and coordination efforts further prepared the Nation to deliver capabilities in each of the five mission areas. Moreover, national exercises (e.g., NLE 2012) and real-world operations (e.g., Sandy) tested existing capabilities and highlighted areas for improvement. A national commitment to analyzing lessons learned from these experiences and integrating results into future operations is critical to the success of the National Preparedness System. These activities become all the more important as the Nation seeks to estimate future capability requirements in a time of constrained resources and increasing complexity and uncertainty.

Looking across all 31 core capabilities outlined in the Goal, the NPR provides a national perspective on critical preparedness trends for whole community partners to inform program priorities, allocate resources, and communicate with stakeholders about issues of shared concern. These trends in national preparedness will become increasingly evident in future reports, as the NPR development process continues to mature and incorporates additional inputs from across the whole community.

Core Capability Definitions

The *National Preparedness Goal* identified 31 core capabilities necessary to achieve success in preparedness, spanning the five mission areas of Prevention, Protection, Mitigation, Response, and Recovery. Three Common core capabilities (Planning; Public Information and Warning; and Operational Coordination) cut across all five mission areas, while four others (Intelligence and Information Sharing; Interdiction and Disruption; and Screening, Search, and Detection; Infrastructure Systems) link to more than one mission area. The core capability definitions published in the Goal and their relevant mission areas appear below.

Common Core Capabilities

Planning: Conduct a systematic process engaging the whole community as appropriate in the development of executable strategic, operational, and/or community-based approaches to meet defined objectives.

Public Information and Warning: Deliver coordinated, prompt, reliable, and actionable information to the whole community through the use of clear, consistent, accessible, and culturally and linguistically appropriate methods to effectively relay information regarding any threat or hazard and, as appropriate, the actions being taken and the assistance being made available.

Operational Coordination: Establish and maintain a unified and coordinated operational structure and process that appropriately integrates all critical stakeholders and supports the execution of core capabilities.

Prevention Core Capabilities

Forensics and Attribution: Conduct forensic analysis and attribute terrorist acts (including the means and methods of terrorism) to their source, to include forensic analysis as well as attribution for an attack and for the preparation for an attack in an effort to prevent initial or follow-on acts and/or swiftly develop counter-options.

Prevention/Protection Core Capabilities

Intelligence and Information Sharing: Provide timely, accurate, and actionable information resulting from the planning, direction, collection, exploitation, processing, analysis, production, dissemination, evaluation, and feedback of available information concerning threats to the United States, its people, property, or interests; the development, proliferation, or use of WMDs; or any other matter bearing on U.S. national or homeland security by Federal, state, local, and other stakeholders. Information sharing is the ability to exchange intelligence, information, data, or knowledge among Federal, state, local, or private sector entities, as appropriate.

Interdiction and Disruption: Delay, divert, intercept, halt, apprehend, or secure threats and/or hazards.

Screening, Search, and Detection: Identify, discover, or locate threats and/or hazards through active and passive surveillance and search procedures. This may include the use of systematic examinations and assessments, sensor technologies, or physical investigation and intelligence.

Protection Core Capabilities

Access Control and Identity Verification: Apply a broad range of physical, technological, and cyber measures to control admittance to critical locations and systems, limiting access to authorized individuals to carry out legitimate activities.

Cybersecurity: Protect against damage to, the unauthorized use of, and/or the exploitation of (and, if needed, the restoration of) electronic communications systems and services (and the information contained therein).

Physical Protective Measures: Reduce or mitigate risks, including actions targeted at threats, vulnerabilities, and/or consequences, by controlling movement and protecting borders, critical infrastructure, and the homeland.

Risk Management for Protection Programs and Activities: Identify, assess, and prioritize risks to inform Protection activities and investments.

Supply Chain Integrity and Security: Strengthen the security and resilience of the supply chain.

Mitigation Core Capabilities

Community Resilience: Lead the integrated effort to recognize, understand, communicate, plan, and address risks so that the community can develop a set of actions to accomplish Mitigation and improve resilience.

Long-term Vulnerability Reduction: Build and sustain resilient systems, communities, and critical infrastructure and key resources lifelines so as to reduce their vulnerability to natural, technological, and human-caused incidents by lessening the likelihood, severity, and duration of the adverse consequences related to these incidents.

Risk and Disaster Resilience Assessment: Assess risk and disaster resilience so that decision makers, responders, and community members can take informed action to reduce their entity's risk and increase their resilience.

Threats and Hazard Identification: Identify the threats and hazards that occur in the geographic area; determine the frequency and magnitude; and incorporate this into analysis and planning processes so as to clearly understand the needs of a community or entity.

Response Core Capabilities

Critical Transportation: Provide transportation (including infrastructure access and accessible transportation services) for response priority objectives, including the evacuation of people and animals, and the delivery of vital response personnel, equipment, and services into the affected areas.

Environmental Response/ Health and Safety: Ensure the availability of guidance and resources to address all hazards including hazardous materials, acts of terrorism, and natural disasters in support of the responder operations and the affected communities.

Fatality Management Services: Provide fatality management services, including body recovery and victim identification, working with state and local authorities to provide temporary mortuary solutions, sharing information with mass care services for the purpose of reunifying family members and caregivers with missing persons/remains, and providing counseling to the bereaved.

Mass Care Services: Provide life-sustaining services to the affected population with a focus on hydration, feeding, and sheltering to those who have the most need, as well as support for reunifying families.

Mass Search and Rescue Operations: Deliver traditional and atypical search and rescue capabilities, including personnel, services, animals, and assets to survivors in need, with the goal of saving the greatest number of endangered lives in the shortest time possible.

On-scene Security and Protection: Ensure a safe and secure environment through law enforcement and related security and protection operations for people and communities located within affected areas and also for all traditional and atypical response personnel engaged in lifesaving and life-sustaining operations.

Operational Communications: Ensure the capacity for timely communications in support of security, situational awareness, and operations by any and all means available, among and between affected communities in the impact area and all response forces.

Public and Private Services and Resources: Provide essential public and private services and resources to the affected population and surrounding communities, to include emergency power to critical facilities, fuel support for emergency responders, and access to community staples (e.g., grocery stores, pharmacies, and banks) and fire and other first response services.

Public Health and Medical Services: Provide lifesaving medical treatment via emergency medical services and related operations and avoid additional disease and injury by providing targeted public health and medical support and products to all people in need within the affected area.

Situational Assessment: Provide all decision makers with decision-relevant information regarding the nature and extent of the hazard, any cascading effects, and the status of the response.

Response/Recovery Core Capabilities

Infrastructure Systems: Stabilize critical infrastructure functions, minimize health and safety threats, and efficiently restore and revitalize systems and services to support a viable, resilient community.

Recovery Core Capabilities

Economic Recovery: Return economic and business activities (including food and agriculture) to a healthy state and develop new business and employment opportunities that result in a sustainable and economically viable community.

Health and Social Services: Restore and improve health and social services networks to promote the resilience, independence, health (including behavioral health), and well-being of the whole community.

Housing: Implement housing solutions that effectively support the needs of the whole community and contribute to its sustainability and resilience.

Natural and Cultural Resources: Protect natural and cultural resources and historic properties through appropriate planning, mitigation, response, and recovery actions to preserve, conserve, rehabilitate, and restore them consistent with post-disaster community priorities and best practices and in compliance with appropriate environmental and historical preservation laws and executive orders.

Acronym List

ADIS	Arrival and Departure Information System
ASCE	American Society of Civil Engineers
ASPCA	American Society for the Prevention of Cruelty to Animals
ASPR	Assistant Secretary for Preparedness and Response
BARDA	Biomedical Advanced Research and Development Authority
C2C	Connecting to Collections
C2CRE	Command and Control CBRN Response Elements
CBRN	Chemical, biological, radiological, and nuclear
CBRNE	Chemical, biological, radiological, nuclear, and explosive
CDC	Centers for Disease Control and Prevention
CERFP	CBRNE Enhanced Response Force Packages
CERT	Community Emergency Response Team
CISO	Chief Information Security Officers
CRI	Cities Readiness Initiative
CRS	Community Rating System
CST	Civil Support Team
DCRF	Defense CBRN Response Force
DHS	U.S. Department of Homeland Security
DMAT	Disaster Medical Assistance Team
DLA	Defense Logistics Agency
DNA	Deoxyribonucleic Acid
DOD	U.S. Department of Defense
DOE	U.S. Department of Energy
DOJ	U.S. Department of Justice
DOT	U.S. Department of Transportation
EAS	Emergency Alert System
EMAC	Emergency Management Assistance Compact
EMS	Emergency Medical Services
EPA	Environmental Protection Agency
EPCRA	Emergency Planning and Community Right-to-Know Act
ESF	Emergency Support Function
EU	European Union
FBI	Federal Bureau of Investigation
FCC	Federal Communications Commission
FDRC	Federal Disaster Recovery Coordinator
FEMA	Federal Emergency Management Agency
FinCEN	Financial Crimes Enforcement Network
FY	Fiscal Year
GAO	Government Accountability Office
GIS	Geographic Information Systems
GSA	General Services Administration
HHS	U.S. Department of Health and Human Services
HPP	Hospital Preparedness Program
HRF	Homeland Response Force
HSPD	Homeland Security Presidential Directive
IDENT	Automated Biometric Identification System
IMLS	Institute of Museum and Library Services
IPAWS	Integrated Public Alert and Warning System
MS-ISAC	Multi-State Information Sharing and Analysis Center
NCCIC	National Cybersecurity and Communications Integration Center
NCIRP	National Cyber Incident Response Plan

NDRF	National Disaster Recovery Framework
NDMS	National Disaster Medical System
NECP	National Emergency Communications Plan
NERC	North American Electric Reliability Corporation
NFIP	National Flood Insurance Program
NGI	Next Generation Identification
NG911	Next Generation 9-1-1
NIMS	National Incident Management System
NIPP	National Infrastructure Protection Plan
NIST	National Institute of Standards and Technology
NLE	National Level Exercise
NOAA	National Oceanic and Atmospheric Administration
NPR	National Preparedness Report
NRCC	National Response Coordination Center
NRDA	Natural Resource Damage Assessment
NRF	National Response Framework
NSA	National Security Agency
NSI	Nationwide Suspicious Activity Reporting Initiative
NTSB	National Transportation Safety Board
ODIC	Office of Disability Integration and Coordination
PHEMCE	Public Health Emergency Medical Countermeasures Enterprise
PHEP	Public Health Emergency Preparedness
PIV	Personal Identity Verification
PIV-I	Personal Identity Verification Interoperability
PPD	Presidential Policy Directive
PSA	Protective Security Advisor
RESTORE	Resources and Ecosystems Sustainability, Tourist Opportunities, and Revived Economy of the Gulf Coast
RISC	Repository for Individuals of Special Concern
Risk MAP	Risk Mapping, Assessment, and Planning
RRAP	Regional Resiliency Assessment Program
RSAT	Risk Self-Assessment Tool
SAR	Search and Rescue
SBA	U.S. Small Business Administration
SLOSH	Sea, Lake, and Overland Surges from Hurricanes
SLTTGCC	State, Local, Tribal, and Territorial Government Coordinating Council
SPR	State Preparedness Report
THIRA	Threat and Hazard Identification and Risk Assessment
TRIPwire	Technical Resource for Incident Prevention
TSA	Transportation Security Administration
US&R	Urban Search and Rescue
USCG	U.S. Coast Guard
USDA	U.S. Department of Agriculture
UFAS	Uniform Federal Accessibility Standards
USACE	U.S. Army Corps of Engineers
USGS	U.S. Geological Survey
USPS	U.S. Postal Service
USSS	U.S. Secret Service
WEA	Wireless Emergency Alerts
WMD	Weapons of Mass Destruction

Endnotes

[1] International Association of Emergency Managers and National Incident Management Systems and Advanced Technologies Institute, "Compendium of Public-private Partnerships for Emergency Management," 2012, http://www.padres-ppp.org/NimsatPPP/resources/Final%20PPP%20Report_101812.pdf.

[2] Trust for America's Health, *Ready or Not? 2012: Protecting the Public from Diseases, Disasters, and Bioterrorism*, December 2012, p. 24, http://healthyamericans.org/report/101/

[3] Rosina Bierbaum, Joel B. Smith, Arthur Lee, Maria Blair, Lynne Carter, F. Stuart Chapin III, Paul Fleming, Susan Ruffo, Missy Stults, Shannon McNeeley, Emily Wasley, and Laura Verduzco, "A comprehensive review of climate adaptation in the United States: more than before, but less than needed," Mitigation and Adaptation Strategies for Global Change March 2013, Volume 18, Issue 3, pp 361-406, http://link.springer.com/article/10.1007/s11027-012-9423-1/fulltext.html.

[4] CTIA-The Wireless Association, "Wireless Emergency Alerts on Your Mobile Device," 2012, http://www.ctia.org/consumer_info/safety/index.cfm/AID/12082.

[5] Deloitte and the National Association of State Chief Information Officers, "2012 Deloitte-NASCIO Cybersecurity Study," 2012, p.3, http://www.deloitte.com/assets/Dcom-UnitedStates/Local%20Assets/Documents/AERS/us_aers_nascio%20Cybersecurity%20Study_10192012.pdf

[6] Ibid., p. 7.

[7] North American Electric Reliability Corporation, "2011 NERC Grid Security Exercise, After Action Report," March 2012.

[8] Earl J. Baker, Kenneth Broad, Jeffrey Czajkowski, Robert Meyer, and Ben Orlov, "Risk Perceptions and Preparedness among Mid-Atlantic Coastal Residents in Advance of Hurricane Sandy," Wharton, University of Pennsylvannia, November 2012, p. 4.

[9] National Research Council, "Tsunami Warning and Preparedness: An Assessment of the U.S. Tsunami Program and the Nation's Preparedness Efforts," National Academy of Sciences, 2011

[10] Associated Press. "After Sandy, officials are wondering what it takes to get people to heed evacuation orders," November 14, 2012, http://www.newser.com/article/da2i0bj80/after-sandy-officials-are-wondering-what-it-takes-to-get-people-to-heed-evacuation-orders.html

[11] Miranda Leitsinger. "The stay-behinds: Residents tell why they ignored mandatory evacuation edict," October 29, 2012, http://usnews.nbcnews.com/_news/2012/10/29/14784392-the-stay-behinds-residents-tell-why-they-ignored-mandatory-evacuation-edict?lite

[12] Jay Baker, Bob Meyer, and Kenny Broad, "Hurricane Earl Real-Time Survey," February, 2012, http://www.nationalevacuationconference.org/files/2012/presentations/day1/Jay_Baker.pdf

[13] "Hurricane Irene Response: A Behind the Scenes Look at New Jersey's First Large-Scale Evacuation in Modern History," February, 2012. http://www.nationalevacuationconference.org/files/2012/presentations/day1/Jon_Carnegie.pdf

[14] Susan L. Cutter, Christopher T. Emrich, Gregg Bowser,Dara Angelo, and Jerry T. Mitchell 2011 South Carolina Hurricane Evacuation Study Behavioral Report: Final Report, August 15, 2011, http://webra.cas.sc.edu/hvri/docs/HES_2011_Final_Report.pdf

[15] National Emergency Management Association, NEMA Biennial Report, 2012, p. 2.

[16] Bipartisan WMD Terrorism Center, "The Bipartisan WMD Terrorism Research Center's Bio-Response Report Card," 2011, pp. 55–58, http://www.wmdcenter.org/wp-content/uploads/2011/10/bio-response-report-card-2011.pdf.

[17] Ibid., p. 58.

[18] Ibid., pp. 55–58.

[19] Crystal Franco and Nidhi Bouri, "Environmental Decontamination Following a Large-scale Bioterrorism Attack: Federal Progress and Remaining Gaps," *Biosecurity and Bioterrorism: Biodefense Strategy, Practice, and Science* 8(2), 2010.

[20] Larry Bedore, "FEMORS 2011 Status Report," Florida Emergency Mortuary Operations Response System, 2012, p. 8, http://www.femors.org/docs/FEMORS_Status_Report_2011.pdf.

[21] New York City Office of Chief Medical Examiner, Unified Victim Identification System (UVIS), 2013.

[22] Erin McLachlan, "Regional Mass Fatality Response System," presented at the National Emergency Management Summit, March 4, 2010, http://www.ehcca.com/presentations/emsummit4/1_01.pdf.

[23] Colleen Pillus, "Dutchess County Hosts Nation's Largest Mass Fatality Training Exercise," Dutchess County Government, New York, May 16, 2012, http://www.co.dutchess.ny.us/CountyGov/Departments/CountyExecutive/21466.htm.

[24] International Association of Emergency Managers and National Incident Management Systems and Advanced Technologies Institute, "Compendium of Public-private Partnerships for Emergency Management," 2012, http://www.padres-ppp.org/NimsatPPP/resources/Final%20PPP%20Report_101812.pdf.

[25] Association of State and Territorial Health Officials (ASTHO), "Budget Cuts Continue to Affect the Health of Americans: Research Brief," August 2012, http://www.astho.org/Research/Data-and-Analysis/ASTHO-Budget-Cuts-Impact-Research-Brief-Update-(August-2012)/

[26] Trust for America's Health, *Ready or Not? 2012: Protecting the Public's Health from Diseases, Disasters, and Bioterrorism*, December 2010, http://healthyamericans.org/assets/files/TFAH2010ReadyorNot%20FINAL.pdf

[27] Trust for America's Health, *Ready or Not? 2012: Protecting the Public's Health from Diseases, Disasters, and Bioterrorism*, December 2012, http://healthyamericans.org/report/101/

[28] Ben Hallman, The Huffington Post, "After Sandy, Communication Breakdown Hampered Efforts To Find Evacuated Seniors," November 16, 2012, http://www.huffingtonpost.com/2012/11/16/sandy-communication-evacuated-seniors_n_2141699.html.

[29] Michael Powell and Sheri Fink, The New York Times, "Nursing Home Is Faulted Over Care After Storm," November 9, 2012, http://www.nytimes.com/2012/11/10/nyregion/queens-nursing-home-is-faulted-over-care-after-storm.html?hp&_r=1&.

[30] American Red Cross, "Social Media in Disasters and Emergencies," 2012, http://www.redcross.org/news/press-release/More-Americans-Using-Mobile-Apps-in-Emergencies.

[31] CNA, "Social Media in Emergency Management: Initial Findings of a 2012 National Survey of Emergency Management Agencies," 2012.

[32] American Society of Civil Engineers, "Failure to Act: The Economic Impact of Current Investment Trends in Water and Wastewater Treatment Infrastructure," 2011, p. 6.

[33] American Society of Civil Engineers, "Failure to Act: The Impact of Current Infrastructure Investment on America's Economic Future," 2013, p. 4.

[34] NYC Business Solutions, "Hurricane Sandy Business Recovery Information," 2012, http://www.nyc.gov/html/sbs/nycbiz/html/home/home.shtml.

[35] The Cedar Rapids Area Chamber of Commerce, "First Business Case Management Program For A Natural Disaster," January 2012.

[36] David M. Abramson, PhD; Yoon Soo Park, MS; Tasha Stehling-Ariza, MPH; Irwin Redlener, MD; American Medical Association, "Children as Bellwethers of Recovery: Dysfunctional Systems and the Effects of Parents, Households, and Neighborhoods on Serious Emotional Disturbance in Children After Hurricane Katrina," August 23, 2010.

[37] National Commission on Children and Disasters, "2010 Report to the President and Congress," October 2010, p. 94.

[38] National Center for Law and Economic Justice, "Brou vs. FEMA Summary," September 26, 2006, http://www.nclej.org/pdf/BrouPressRelease.pdf

[39] Federal Register, "Americans with Disabilities Act (ADA) and Architectural Barriers Act (ABA) Accessibility Guidelines; Emergency Transportable Housing Units," June 18, 2012, http://www.access-board.gov/eth/nprm.htm.